SISA'S VI
A Radical I
of Jo:

E. SAN JUAN, Jr.

Philippines Cultural Studies Center
Connecticut, USA

Copyright © E. San Juan, Jr. 2014
All rights reserved

ISBN-13: 978-1499165180
ISBN-10: 1499165188

The chapter, "Sisa's Vengeance," was first presented as a paper for the Rizal 150 International Conference, University of the Philippines, June 2011; a version was published in Kritika Kultura, August 2011; included here is the latest revision. Reprinted 2014.

CONTACT: philcsc@gmail.com
philcsc@sbcglobal.net

CONTENTS

Foreword *4*

I. Rizal and Revolution in the Age of Imperial Terrorism *26*

II. Sisa's Vengeance: Rizal & the "Woman Question *65*

Rizal the Feminist: A Review *116*
by Francis C. Macansantos

FOREWORD

A specter is haunting *las islas Filipinas*—not just the territory, but also the Filipino diaspora around the world. Jose Rizal as ghost or the phantom in the neocolonial opera stalks across islands and continents. Rizal--the name is familiar, even a household word, like Avenida Rizal, Rizal Coliseum, the "Rizal" brand attached to all kinds of souvenirs, gewgaws, and collectibles. But over the decades and centuries, after 150 years, somehow the figure remains distant, alien, self-estranged. Rizal, the national hero, is routinely celebrated by bureaucrats, cult-followers, trendy pundits and inutile academics. But among so many fetishized images, counterfeit icons, and fabrications, who is the "real" and "true" Rizal? Such a question is perhaps anachronistic, irrelevant, or foolish in our postmodern age of simulacras, hybrid replicas, and virtual dissimulations. Our task in such a bind is to explore the nexus of duplicities and contradictions in our vexed and vexatious question.

Rizal's significance for us today remains problematic, contentious, open-ended. His prestige is no longer monolithic, unequivocal, standardized. Readers of his works are now prone to extract multiple ambiguous meanings. After Constantino's signal interrogation of the ascribed heroism of Rizal, we are left to puzzle out the gap between public appearance and covert essence, between the transparent integrity and the extravagant dissonance of our subject. Unamuno's impression of a quixotic, Hamlet-like Rizal still appears warranted, despite the efforts of Ambeth Ocampo, Malou Jacob, and others to restore him to his all-too-human dimension. Nonetheless, Rizal remains unique and extraordinary in his single-minded commitment to his people's liberation. Deconstructing the Empire's transcendental signified, he had to construct the people/nation with a distinct "personality," a world-historic presence, one no longer needing tutelage and capable of self-governance. This was a collective project of contriving a social contract by mobilizing *potentia multitudine* (Spinoza) in the process of permanent revolution, activating popular memory to midwife the future.

One of Rizal's protagonists in the *Fili* posited the rationale of his life-long endeavor (*conatus*): "A life not consecrated to a great ideal is a useless one... Redemption presumes virtue; virtue presumes sacrifice; sacriffice presumes love." The logic of such a syllogism led to Rizal's arrest, trial, and execution. He was lucky to be able to chose the form of his death despite the peril of misrecognitions and misrepresentations. As Fr. Miguel Bernad (1998) has lucidly shown, Rizal's trial was his vindication; the Court's judgment was already presupposed in his being invidiously categorized as an "Indio." More scandalous was Rizal's habit of identifying himself with all the victims of colonialism, whether *Indios*, Chinese, creoles, ethnic aborigines, or marginalized Spanish peninsulars, thus articulating the syntagm of particular grievances into a universal cry of revolt against global injustice, a paradigmatic agenda of rectification and settling of accounts. "Sisa's vengeance" is the shibboleth and trope of this agenda.

What above all distinguishes Rizal's sensibility is the habit of thinking dialectically, grasping the total flow of experience in its manifold determinations. In his critique of Morga's chronicle, for instance, he charted a mutable field of passions, affects, contingencies. Beyond the empirical and the aesthetic realms, his concern was always profoundly ethical and humanistic as he negotiated the transition from feudal corporatism to the possessive individualism of bourgeois/market capitalism. In a letter to Mariano Ponce, he considered all the persecutions, cruelties, abuses as necessary for Filipinos to prove their fortitude and valor, so that "in spite of everything and everybody, they will be worthy of liberty....In every struggle there must be victims, and it is the greatest of battles which are the most sanguinary. What is imprisonment? What is death? An illness sends us to bed at times and takes our life. The question is whether this infirmity and this death will afterwards be useless for those who survive" (*Epistolario* 2, 165-66). This challenge to wager life, Rizal affirmed, will generate the missing "personality" of the masses, a desideratum for deserving freedom and independence.

On the Edge of Extra-territorial Musings

Disruptions, aporias, and detours accompanied Rizal's pedagogical and agit-prop vocation. Through his own improvised "ruses of reason," Rizal opposed not only obscurantism and idolatry but also nihilist skepticism and self-deluded egotism. He repeated to his sisters that his motivation in his Enlightenment work was not meant to cause "the stain of dishonor," rather the opposite. His attitude to Marcelo del Pilar and other expatriates in Madrid demonstrated Rizal's conscientious prudence (he later denounced this exorbitant prudence as a native flaw preventing initiatives) in putting honor, construed as the fidelity to principles and national ideals, above mere creature comforts and self-serving welfare: "My politics is to become eclipsed....I wish to be sure that I may never be regarded as a stumbling block to anybody, even though this involves my own fall." Representing himself (in the name of others, justice, the emancipated future) entailed self-erasure, temporizing, ultimately death.

Rizal's sensitivity concerning his personal dignity or honor may be deemed subtly narcissistic, even self-ingratiating. On the other hand, it can also be assayed as a symptom of inadequacy, a gnawing sense of lack, an obsessive preoccupation with an unstable, precarious, nascent selfhood—more precisely, a fallibilistic modality of performing self-determination. That paradox sustained him in straitened circumstances and at the same time undermined his psychic equilibrium. Everything seems pregnant with its contrary (to echo Marx's quip of 1856). Thus he had to laugh to salvage spoiled intentions and damaged ideals. That gave him the formula for thought-experiments, for savage allegory and satire. What is certain is that we need to reject the methological individualism of the liberal/official assessment of Rizal's significance that vitiates many research projects on Rizal designed for advancing fundamentalist programs and/or mercantile self-aggrandizement.

Uncannily, Rizal was a performance artist *avant la lettre*, unwittingly, without premeditation. It was part of a ritualized genre of caring for the soul, inflected from St. Ignatius' exercises and ritualized in the book Rizal had in prison, Thomas a Kempis' *The Imitation of Christ* (see his criticism of Barrantes on theater [1984, 116-24]). Rizal displayed this in countless letters where he dramatized his own imagined part in the campaign for decolonization. In a letter to del Pilar, Rizal exhorted his comrades to inaugurate a more militant policy of courage and genuine solidarity: "Our fellow counrymen, at seeing our valor, at seeing that Rizal is not the exception but the general rule, will also take new courage and lose their fear; there is nothing like example.... God and Destiny are on our side because we have justice and right and because we struggle not for ourselves but for the sacred love we hold for our country and for our fellow countrymen." Earlier he wrote Mariano Ponce to advise Graciano Lopez Jaena to return to the Philippines (instead of going to Cuba, which Rizal later chose to do in order to escape the desperate vicissitudes of his banishment) "to allow himself to be lled in defense of his ideals; we have only once to die, and if we do not die well, we lose an opportunity which will not again be presented to us." He seized that opportunity, the *mise en scéne* for conjuring his avatars and their vestal consorts.

Every commentator shares the consensus that the 1872 martyrdom of Father Burgos, Gomez and Zamora (just a year after the historic inauguration of the Paris Commune) transformed Rizal into a *filibustero*, as he confided to Blumentritt and Ponce. This is the "culprit" who constructed the baroque worlds of the *Noli and Fili*; the latter novel he dedicated to the three martyrs. Anxious to prove himself a worthy heir to the model of his predecessors, Rizal upheld the anagogic idea of vengeance —Simoun/Ibarra's justice cognized as a collective mode of fulfilling a promise to ancestors to heal the rupture of interrupted group exchanges--as the legitimizing foundation of a nation-in-the-making. It is an organic concept of the emergent nation instantiated, as Rizal mindful of the Messiah once put it, wherever two Filipinos are gathered in memory of their birthplace and its common good. He declared: "At the sight of these injustices and cruelties, even as a child my imagination was awakened and I swore to dedicate my life to avenge so many victims; and it is with this idea that I have been studying. This may be seen in all my works and writings; God give me the opportunity some day to carry out my promise!" Here Rizal was enacting Simoun/Ibarra's role, remembering *inter alia* the blow he received from a *guardia civil* in his youth, the brutal treatment of his mother by the local authorities, and the harrowing mass eviction of his family from their home in Calamba (the details of the agony was conveyed to Rizal in a letter from his sister Narcisa [*Epistolario* V, 167). Clearly, his aspiration to collect what's due, redress grievances, and complete the exchange was nourished and cultivated early on in the hero's tortuous adventure.

Pathos of Incommensurable Desire

After demythologizing the icon, what remains? The protocols for re-interrogating the Rizal cult/hero-worship have been formulated by the recurrent themes and motifs of the major biographies (Palma, Guerrero, Coates, Baron Fernandez). Except for the retraction and the Josephine Bracken episode, most events in Rizal's life are no longer controversial. I consider the *Memorias*, the canonical two novels, certain letters, and the substantive essays central to the understanding of Rizal's import and serviceability for the national-democratic struggle. Of vital importance are those originally written in Tagalog as well as the unfinished and fragmentary manuscripts.

A strategy to decenter the i*lustrado* reformist assessment of Rizal should begin with the letter to the Malolos women, the *Liga Filipina*, the letters to Blumentritt, Ponce and other colleagues in *La Solidaridad,* the unfinished novel on the Tagalog nobility, *Makamisa*, and the two political testaments dated June 20, 1892, entrusted to Dr. Lorenzo Marques for safekeeping. What is confirmed is that Rizal's December 15 manifesto, a guileful recalcitrant document, was never made public. Hidden transcripts and oracular scenarios characterize the operations of the Rizal writing-machine. Between the *Memorias*, the two novels, the commentary on Morga, the major discourses on indolence and the future of the country, his voluminous correspondence, poems such as "Ultimo Adios" and "Mi Retiro," the open letter to the

Malolos women, and the two testaments, etc.--this constellation or network of representamens (to use C.S. Peirce's term for signifiers) delimiting the range of subject-positions the Rizal persona or actant can perform fixes the parameters of further speculation on his usefulness in the task of constructing a popular-democratic bloc, a grass-roots constituency, in the fight for national-popular hegemony. We shift from archaelogy to genealogy: the author dies to give way to a kindred reader/interpreter born in the interstices of his texts and acts, as well as in their rhizomatic ramifications.

There is no question that Rizal's prodigious commitment in trying to represent an emergent nation/people is unprecedented in the annals of the "third world." His identity has been equated with the singular dedication to the liberation of his country which inexorably led to his persecution and martyrdom. On the testimony of Andres Bonifacio and the 1896 generation, and of *ilustrado* politicians from Aguinaldo, Quezon, Roxas, and biographers Wenceslao Retana, Rafael Palma, Austin Craig, Carlos Quirino, Leon Ma. Guerrero, and others, Rizal's heroism is unparalleled in the annals of Philippine history, and of Asia as well. His influence has extended beyond Asia up to the Americas, Europe and Africa. With the usual qualifications, he is now cited together with Ho Chi Minh, Mao Zedong, Gandhi, Sun Yat-Sen. Jose Marti, and other revolutionary nationalists of the last century.

But aside from being a national-democratic intellectual ahead of his time, Rizal and the narrative of his labors constitute a difficult imaginary organon for Filipinos. It is one that occupies a subterranean space transcending historical determinations precisely because of the specific circumstances that defined and circumscribed his life. The saga of his words and deeds symbolizes a specific Filipino modernity that breaks the boundaries of the Enlightenment schematics of ascetic virtue precisely because of its archaic and feudal, even primitive, ingredients. The Rizal mind-body complex may be conceived as the locus for the convergence of heterogeneous socioeconomic formations that by their mixture yields that configuration of an anti-hero first glimpsed by Unamuno and observed by Teodoro Agoncillo, Ante Radaic, Claro Recto, Dolores Feria, and others. In my book *Rizal in Our Time* (Anvil, revised edition 2011), I called attention to some discordant, incongruous elements in the Rizal archive in the hope of synthesizing them. In the two essays collected here, the play of contradictions and seemingly irreconcilable polarities is foregrounded and used as speculative points of departure.

The Indio Witness Speaking Tongues

Rizal's life registers both acquiescence to fate (divine providence, "bathala na/bahala na" = let the overarching plot unfold) and resistance to it. Destiny for Rizal was a contrapuntal orchestration of fatalism and voluntarism. resignation and the affirmation of will-to-power. His project of shaping his life-world was premised on the inertia of circumstances outside his control non-synchronized with occasions for seizing opportunities. His contacts with liberal European intellectuals were such occasions; the other was his meeting with the "Irish half-caste," Josephine Bracken. Rizal's life may be summed up as one unrelenting endeavor to grasp and master, unavailingly, the discourse of the Other. In the process, the Other metamorphosed into multiple worldly others, the sacred merging with the secular: his family, friends, teachers, comrades in *La Solidaridad*, allies in the international conversation (Blumentritt, Meyer, Virchow, etc.). He disavowed this project of comprehending the Other by the power of his sincerity and utter self-abnegation. One proof may be found in his unprecedented letters to the Jesuit "inquisitor" Fr. Pablo Pastells who tried to re-convert him to the orthodox piety of his youth. Rizal sums up his position: "My sole wish is to do what is possible, what is in my hands, the most necessary" (11 November 1892). Despite being commonsensical, down-to-earth and pragmatic, Rizal suffered numerous attacks of depression, profound melancholy, even despair. His diary and letters attest to this cycle of intense moods and dispositions foreshadowing the "wild justice" (Francis Bacon) symptomatic of the compulsion to resurrect the past in order to redeem the present and the future.

The Spanish doctor-biographer Baron Fernandez has highlighted for us the occurrence of those moments. The traces of their beginning can be discerned all throughout the *Memorias* as silences, ellipses, absences that punctuate his departures and returns: from his early sojourn in Binan to the years in Ateneo and UST (1872-1882) and to the first voyage to Europe (1882-1887), and its aftermath. Even the brief interlude (1888) of his travel across the United States—from the quarantine in San Francisco to his comment on America as the land of opportunity despite the lack of civil rights for African Americans—betokened revealing lapses and inconsistencies. Throughout his second foray into Europe, the crisis of his family's plight in Calamba hounded him. Somehow filled with remorse, he blamed himself for his family's eviction from their farmland, the chief source of their livelihood, by the Dominican order; for the persecution and banishment of his relatives, and the suffering of his parents and sisters. He too suffered, feeling himself complicit in causing their misery. On one day in Madrid, June 24, 1884, before the banquet at which he delivered his famous speech honoring Juan Luna and Felix Resurreccion Hidalgo, the starving Rizal was on the verge of delirium.

One contributing factor in Rizal's saturnine if not morbid outlook during that period is the illness brought about by malnutrition, anguished work, and excessive gymnastics, as diagnosed by his good friend Dr. Maximo Viola. In 1886, Viola offered a symptomatology: "Afternoon fevers preceded by chills, slight cough, feeling of fatigue and haggardness" (Baron Fernandez 1980. 95). Rizal took arsenic and discontinued his physical regimen. While emphasizing the material determinants of the psyche, we will not pursue a mechanistic Freudian analysis such as Radaic's , or the ludicruous Lombroesque portrayal of Rizal carried out by Retana (1979).

Rizal believed in every person's capacity to learn from mistakes and solve problems, developing in the process an informed and intelligent will-power. Creative human labor, the metabolism of social praxis, is the key to the fashioning of culture; solidarity or cooperation is the basis for the making of civilization. At the same time, Rizal intuited Marx's cardinal axiom that individuality (sensuous praxis) is nothing but the totality of social relations at a specific time and place of one's existence. Human agency becomes possible and materially efficacious only within the limits established by the historical parameters of possibility, which in turn is configured by the degree of development of the productive forces, by the prevailing division of social labor and its ideological legitimization vis-à-vis the totality of social relations of production and reproduction. The body, sexuality and difference, as well as the registers of shifting identities, acquire their meanings and resonance within this totality. This hypothesis can be tested and judged in the crucible of revolutionary social praxis.

The doctor we quoted earlier is the same Viola who accompanied Rizal in a "grand tour" of Europe in 1887, up to the memorable visit to that Viennese siren—one of the *manggagaway*s that Rizal dared to experiment with, prior to his Dapitan exile and the confrontation with sorcery and/or psychosomatic illness. He was immune to seduction because of wounds sustained earlier; the scars of the Katigbak affair (replicated in the Leonor Rivera showdown) were still raw. Rizal's act of memorializing in his journals those temptations performed the rite of exorcism. The next documented attack of depression occurred after his stay in Biarritz, his refusal to accept Nelly Boustead's condition (excusing it with the phrase "we are all in the hands of God" or Fate), the completion of *El Filibusterismo*, aggravated by the schisms among his friends in Madrid, and the news in 1891 that the Madrid Supreme Court upheld the punishment suffered by the people of Calamba. Before he left for Hong Kong, Rizal was suicidal. He wrote to his friend Jose Ma. Basa: "…for I may die, or something may happen to me, and I don't want you to lose anything in case I cannot embark. I fear that something may happen and I may not go through with the trip" (Baron Fernandez 1980, 195-96). Melancholia and mourning for the lost "object"—the extra-territorial *patria*, youth's innocence--triggered shame that eventually deteriorated into guilt and self-blame.

Mapping Disenchantment and Epiphany

Such existential ordeals were not new for Rizal. They accompanied the dissolution of the inherited religious world-view, the traditional *pietas* of classical antiquity, and its replacement by a secular, worldly orientation. The therapeutic reflections on the dangers of uprooting, nostalgic longing, confrontation with new hostile environments, and the failure of vows and promises, are poignantly recorded in the *Memorias* and intimate letters to his family, friends, and collaborators. His studies of physics and philosophy precipitated a "polarization" that "plunged me into a world of miseries from which I have not yet emerged." In his youth he endured the agony of his isolation in Binan and Manila. But such traumatic paroxysms were nothing compared to the lethal void sprung from the vertigo of amorous fantasy catalyzed by the figure of Segunda Katigbak. Death and the erotic constituted the hero's passive/active, oscillating, precariously balanced sensibility. The chapter in *Memorias* between April to December 1877 constitutes a signifying chain of tropes, images, and metaphoric clusters that capture the destruction of the phallogocentric subject (earlier fed by Ateneo medals and his parents' support) and the passage through a fleeting *jouissance* in the moment of loss, speechlessness, and motor paralysis. Rizal was devastated. Ironically, representation (writing) equals loss of self-presence, amnesia, a leap into the abyss. The subject becomes other and drastically re-positioned through this break, this fade-out and seizure—a bewitchment he would analyze during his exile. This disintegration (ec-stasis) of the psyche transpires in a fantasy game combining disavowal and complicity, alternating ingenious retreats and disingenuous advances.

We witness here the inscription of the psyche into the tabooed space of mourning, frontier-crossing or violations of borders, and the uncanny haunting of the ruined home. The ruptured ego experiences the pleasure of its vertigo as Rizal anticipates the final disappearance of the beloved several days before the last meeting: "That was the first night that I felt an anguish and inquietude resembling love, if not jealousy, perhaps because I saw that I was separating from her, perhaps because a million obstacles would stand between us, so that my budding love was increasing and seemed to be gaining vigor in the flight" (Zaide and Zaide 1984, 314). The climactic separation is rehearsed here as though it would relieve, if not prevent, the advent of that catastrophic eventuality. The lover's mind is already crippled as he waited for the appearance of the vehicle where the beloved's handkerchief will appear as a premonitory sign: "I saw the swift currents [of a nearby brook] carrying away branches that they tore from the bushes and my thought, wandering in other regions and having other subjects, paid no attention to them." Finally the moment arrives and the erotic object enters the horizon of ethical decision—only to find the agent-to-be immobilized, even castrated, despite a histrionic stance and theatrical readiness:

…She bowed to me smiling and waving her handkerchief, I just lifted up my head and said nothing. Alas! Such has always happened to me in the most painful moments of my life. My tongue, profuse talker, becomes dumb when my heart is bursting with feelings. The vehicle passed like a swift shadow, leaving no other trace but a horrible void in the world of my affections…. [I]n the critical moments of my life, I have always acted against my will, obeying different purposes and mighty doubts. i goaded my horse and took another road without having chosen it, exclaiming: This is ended thus. Ah, how much truth, how much meaning, these words then had! My youthful and trusting love ended! The first hours of my first love ended. My virgin heart will forever weep the risky step it took in the abyss covered with flowers. My illusion will return, indeed, but indifferent, incomprehensible, preparing me for the first deception on the road of grief. (Zaide and Zaide 1984, 317).

Subversive Metamorphosis

That experience would prove deracinating and purgative for the adolescent Rizal. In order to cure himself, more precisely rescue the mortified ego from further "deception", he tried to deflect the libidinal drive to fix its cathexis on another woman, L, an older bachelor girl, "fair with seductive and attractive eyes"; but his thoughts and heart followed Segunda Katigbak "through the night to her town." This excursion to a substitute failed to heal the wound, pushing him to the edge of perverse self-immolation and necrophilia: "If the most filthy corpse had told me that she too was thinking of me, I would have kissed it out of gratitude." Conversely, in the last farewell, the dead lover would release the enslaved mother(land) elegized in "Kundiman" and cohabit with her in "enchanted terrain." Rehearsing the agony of loss, the prodigal son/lover would later on reflect on this episode in order to equip himself for the ordeal of the last destination.

Overall, the admonitory impact of this experience—a recapitulation of abjecthood necessary for acquiring a new subjectivity—should not be overestimated. I submit that the truly crippling trauma for Rizal was his four-years deportation to Dapitan following the blasting of his hope that Governor Despujol would allow the settlement of his family to British North Borneo. This was wholly unexpected, in spite of earlier events such as the deportation of his relatives (in particular, Manuel Hidalgo) and the painful uprooting of the Rizal clan from Calamba and their temporary stay in Hong Kong. Apart from this exile (1892-1896) culminating in his arrest in the middle of his travel to Cuba, speedy trial and execution, the other profound crisis in Rizal's life (as already mentioned) was the arrest and extremely cruel treatment of his mother for alleged connivance with his uncle Jose Alberto in trying to kill his delinquent wife. This happened a year before the 1872 Cavite Mutiny and the execution of the priests Burgos, Gomez and Zamora; and the retreat of his brother Paciano Rizal from public visibility. Rizal recounted this vicious treatment of his mother in the third chapter of his *Memorias*, a primal scene of horror—even though the vile torturer suffered remorse.

The case lasted for two and a half years. The thirteen-year old child identified with his mother, victim of an iniquitous system resembling that suffered by the protagonist of Alexandre Dumas' *The Count of Monte Cristo* that Rizal was reading then, together with Chateaubriand's melodramatic romances. Teodora Alonzo's brutalization and the murder of Father Burgos coalesced to make Rizal a "filibustero." In this context, Rizal's novels may be conceived as a sustained, elaborate program of therapy to overcome the earlier traumas of abjection and refusal. However, the Dapitan calamity could not be resolved except by martyrdom which Rizal welcomed, having anticipated that ending a long time ago in his dreams and his counter-intuitive deciphering of the maneuvers of the Jesuit priests and the Katipunan messengers.

Burlesque Dance of the Enigma

Reviewing in 1901 the publication of Rizal's *Noli* translated into English, the "father" of American realism William Dean Howells unreservedly praised its exquisite artistry. It reminded him of the verbal economy of modern Spanish novelists; indeed, Rizal "has gone beyond them in a certain sparing touch, with which he presents situation and character by mere statement of fact, without explanation or comment" (1901, 805). Is Howells reading the same artifact charged by many to be melodramatic, weirdly baroque, sentimental, replete with prolix moralizing, etc.? It seems that, for the Yankee reviewer, this "little saffron man" succeeded in rendering types "with unerring delicacy and distinctness." We suspect that Howell is compensating for the barbaric aggression of Generals Otis and Arthur McArthur's soldiers, climaxing in the ferocious pacification campaign of Generals Bell and Smith, during the Filipino-American War (1899-1902); this genocidal horror was recently recalled to an American public by John Sayles' film, *Amigo,* without mention of 1.4 milion dead Filipinos. Rizal's "unimpeachable veracity," for Howell, resides in "the self-control of the artistic spirit" shown "even in the extreme of apparent caricature" (1901, 806).

We forego summarizing the two novels here. Needless to say, a historical materialist perspective goes beyond the mere inventory of facts and statistics, requiring the deployment of situational frames and intertextual contexts. Linkages and connections are needed in order to grasp the totality of any phenomenon. In addition to the empiricist gloss, we need a versatile semiotic reading of the Rizal archive responsive to its polysemous texture/structure. Rizal, however, would surely repudiate the cosmopolitanesque, free-floating notion of Filipino-as-Everyman, Patricia Evangelista's notorious denizen of a borderless world, the anonymous *balikbayan* giving back to the country what she has purchased/earned from servitude to the rich nation-states of the Global North (*Pinoy Abrod* 2004). Rizal is much more skeptical, less naïve, than our well-intentioned but nonetheless naively cynical compatriots. This is in keeping with his own self-reflexive hermeneutic, a rigorous interrogation of the motives of his words and actions and their resonance in varying constellations of forces and events.

There is no questioning Rizal's obsessive engagement with constructing the Filipino as a nascent collective agency, the foundation for a new polity based on rational argumentation and civic virtues. He explored the possibilities immanent in the immediate present, invested with contradictory tendencies and implications. As Rafael Palma and others have demonstrated, Rizal's singularity inheres in this intransigent focus on his mission: "I prefer the death of the ant which bites even in the moment of dying....I am going to prove to those who deny patriotism to us that we know how to die for our duty and our convictions" (Palma 1949, 340). Gladiator-like, he challenged the Furies, staking everything, claiming the righteous God on his side.

Rizal's trenchant self-esteem, the antidote to pride, was paradoxically a self-negating virtue. Sacrificing his life, rejecting conservative prudence and welcoming death in the arena, Rizal pursued his writerly task, his shamanistic duty, to expose the cancerous bodies of the afflicted on the steps of the temple so that others—presumably the healthy, compassionate ones-- may offer a remedy. Rizal staged the illusion of this spectacle in the narratives of his two novels, as well as in various satirical pieces. They operated as prophylactic devices of purgation, salutary vehicles of exorcism. The "shock and awe" triggered by obscurantist terror was rendered intelligible from the optic of a curative agent/shaman, the culture-hero of folk memory and autochtonous tradition. Rizal crafted the spectacle of this crisis, with its catharsis involving both victimizers and victims, under the sign of an avenging spirit that is the mother of all revolts and transgressions:

> Some people say: It is these imprisonments and deaths that terrify and intimidate the rest!" If the country lacks courage, if it is paralyzed by despair, infected, close to disorganization, fire is precisely the remedy indicated. Fire will awaken vitality, irritate the cells, cause the fluids to circulate…And it is only dead if there exists no vitality at all. Suppose we free it today from the tyranny of the friars; tomorrow it will fall under the tyranny of their employees (Epistolario 2, 166).

Insurgency Without Guarantees

Slaves of today, the tyrants of tomorrow—are we hearing echoes of the fugitive Ibarra? of the prophet-demystifier Tasio? The self-embattled Rizal feared the return of the repressed embodied, for instance, in Simoun, the personification of the irrationality of the whole system. So he speculated that this prophecy can be foiled by critique, by vigilant self-scrutiny and anatomizing of the body politic. In the process, Voltairean metaphysics yielded to Dionysian actuality. This incarnation or transubstantiation of ideas may have resulted only in "Felipinas Caliban," as Alma Jill Dizon argues in her allegorical reading of the two female protagonists, Dona Victorina and Dona Consolacion. Like Fr. John Schumacher (1978), Dizon calls attention to Rizal's criticism of the corruption of complicitous subjects. But such individual cases cannot be divorced from the brutalized plight of the whole body politic.

Rizal was unsparing in applying self-disciplinary measures. Based on his own experience, he reminded the Malolos women how Filipina obsequiousness arose from "the combined effect of their excessive kindness, modesty, and perhaps ignorance." As Rizal noted in diagnosing subaltern indolence, the malaise resulted from centuries of slave/master inter-dependency whose idealist phenomenology Marx and Engels had stood on its head in their critique of Hegel's *Philosophy of Right (1970)* and *The Holy Family* (1844;1975). Unfortunately, this one-sided view of Rizal's partisanship needs to be rectified by a more nuanced, holistic appraisal of the multifaceted world of both artifices in which all the characters are embedded. Like Sisa, both women function as indices of a much broader dynamic typicality, what Engels had in mind when he theorized the concept of scrupulous realism in his remarks on Balzac, Lasalle, Ibsen, and other works (1973).

Praised by Howells (as noted earlier), Rizal's critical realism was premised on an analysis of the total situation embracing both colonized and colonizer. Engaged in subverting delusions/illusions, he paid close attention to the complicities of the colonized with her subjection. Mapping the trajectory of decolonization (as voiced in Tasio's jeremiads, in Elias' predicament, or in the tragic ambiguities of Cabesang Tales and his clan), Rizal sought to forge a national-popular will that would interweave European ideas and the vernacular canon, folk millenarian impulses and elite intellectual resources. We can cite the hermeneutic insight of another scholar, Eugenio Matibag, who examines in a more dialectical manner the "play of an emancipatory desire" in Rizal's novels. While he remarks on the bifurcations and antitheses of characters and motifs, Matibag asserts that Rizal believed in a "unique Philippine culture...founded on a Filipino creolism" (1995, 262). Hence Rizal "creolizes Spanish language by including regionalisms, Tagalog words and Philippine spellings in dialogue and narration." Indeed, the novels are genuinely intertextual and analogic, eliciting a wide spectrum of responses and thus anticipating the magic realism of Gabriel Garcia Marquez and other postmodern fabulists. What I would propose, however, is the application of the method of metacommentary (exemplified in the works of Walter Benjamin, Bertolt Brecht, Fredric Jameson) that combines a critique of ideology with a heuristic exploration of utopian, carnivalesque possibilities. After all, the actualities of the future are present in the interregnum of what exists but not-yet, in the pedagogical domain of potentiality, as well as in the quotidian experience of our shared, interactive lives.

Anti-Climactic Caesura: From Dapitan to Fort Santiago

When Rizal was accused during his trial of instigating the *Katipunan* rebellion that prematurely exploded in

August 1896, he denied it and was compelled to issue the December 15 manifesto. We take note of the countervailing forces that bracket the sincerity of this document. Constantino and other iconoclasts focus on Rizal's denunciation of the rebellion and his appeal for reforms from above as proof of Rizal's counter-revolutionary if not assimilationist sentiment. This text, plus his response to Dr. Pio Valenzuela's visit to Dapitan in July 1896, became self-incriminatory despite the Katipunan's extolling of Rizal as the charismatic progenitor of the insurrection. Earlier Rizal confessed that the *Liga* which he planned in 1892, four years before his arrest, was "stillborn." During his exile in Dapitan, Rizal met Josephine Bracken via the visit of Hong Kong citizen George Taufer. Eventually she became his common-law wife despite the initial antipathy of his mother and sisters. Bracken's miscarriage and Rizal's burial of his unborn child Francisco (named after his father) is interpreted by Austin Coates as symbolic of Rizal's life as "futureless as the child....For once he had succumbed to his desires, and this was weakness, and he knew it" (1992, 273; see Ofilada 2003, 46-48). A weakness that Rizal acknowledged? Scarcely. In his letters pleading that the Rizal clan show some kindness to Bracken, Rizal wrote (to his sister Trinidad, 21 Nov. 1895): "I am convinced that she [Josephine] is better than what they say. What she does for me, how she obeys me and attends to me, would not have been done to me by a Filipina" (quoted in Ofilada 2003, 43; see also Rodolfo 1958). Physical coercion was futile without ideological pressure. Given the surveillance, threat of assassination, and unrelenting persuasive moves—symbolic violence immanent in the carceral networks of biopower and the despotic "distribution of the sensible" (to borrow Jacques Ranciere's phrase)--imposed on Rizal in Dapitan, the refuge afforded by Bracken's companionship could not be ignored for reasons of *delicadeza*. In his "last farewell" (first published in Antonio Luna's revolutionary newspaper *La Independencia* in 25 September 1898), the pilgrim-voyager Rizal finally acknowledged the help of *dulce extranjera* [Josephine Bracken]. bidding farewell to "my joy,...the sweet friend that lightened my way."

As proposed in the essays that follow, a revaluation of Rizal and a more all-encompassing appraisal of his contribution to our national-democratic revolution may be initated by using Rizal's Dapitan exile as its center of gravity, the site of interxtuality, dialogue, and experimental inquiry. It might serve as the theoretical crucible for decoding the themes of difference, sexuality, and subjectivity along the signifying web of discursive practices and institutions that make up our colonial and neocolonial history. To be sure, the patriarch-oriented Rizal was not a feminist or woman-liberationist. But he protested against frailocracy as the epitome of the gender-based authoritarian system, inspired by populist Jacobin ideals, by the classic Roman virtues of Cicero and republican thinkers (Spinoza, Schiller), and by the naturalist, humanist secularism which he absorbed in his European travels (Miguel Morayta once invited Rizal to a celebration of Giordana Bruno in Madrid). His didactic-polemical gloss on the Malolos women's plan to open a night-school is the crucial testimony to his egalitarian conviction that in the process supported unleashing women's energies for a universal program of emancipation traversing the domains of race, class, gender, and nationality. The sixth precept distills that provocative animus to level authoritarian hierarchies: "All men are born equal, naked, without bonds." The paramount injunction is to use the faculty of critical judgment to grasp what is reasonable and just and truthful as we proceed through "the garden of learning," thwarting deceit and enjoying the fruits of mutual aid, convivial reciprocity, in a life of freedom and enjoyment of each other's company.

A Message from the "Belly of the Beast"

Our national beginning may be said to enjoy a permanently resourceful matrix in Rizal's life-work mediated by the 1896 revolution and the protracted resistance to US occupation. We can discount or ignore Rizal, but he will not ignore us. Death for Rizal was a momentary catching of breath before renewed mobilization: "To die is to rest...." Subjectivation followed subjection, dissensus superseded consensus: the model student became a pariah, exile, prisoner, and executed filibustero. Rizal himself provides a fitting epilogue to his life in the last paragraph of his homily to the Malolos women. He evokes the utopian garden of delights, a pastoral milieu of sensuous joy sprung from social labor overcoming the alienation of urban civilization. He conjures for us a vision of truth and rapture, rationality fused with convivial pleasure emanating from solidarity and communal sacrifice:

"Tubo ko'y dakila sa puhunang pagod" at mamatamisin ang ano mang mangyari, ugaling upa sa sino mang mangahas sa ating bayang magsabi ng tunay. Matupad nawa and inyong nasang matuto at hari na ngang sa halamanan ng karununga'y huwag makapitas ng bungang bubut, kundi ang kikitli'y piliiin, pag-isipin muna, lasapin bago lunukin, sapagkat sa balat ng lupa lahat ay haluan, at di bihirang magtanim ang kaaway ng damong pansira, kasama sa binhi sa gitna ng linang ["My profit will be greater than the capital invested"; and I shall gladly accept the usual reward of all who dare tell our people the truth. May your desire to educate yourself be crowned with success; may you in the garden of learning gather not bitter, but choice fruit, looking well before you eat, because on the surface of the globe all is deceit, and often the enemy sows weeds in your seedling plot (1984, 332).

Written in 1889 two years after the publication of the *Noli* (1887), while engaged in annotating *Morga's Sucesos de las Islas Filipinas* (1609), the Malolos epistle illustrates Rizal's conviction that what is needed to redeem the homeland was not a literary man but a good citizen who would deploy heart and head, not yet the force of arms. Before the frontal assault on the Spanish behemoth, a war of maneuver is necessary. Employing both head and heart, the resident of the *polis* would utilize the pen as the principal instrument without preempting the tactical use of other weapons. He reminds fellow agitator Ponce (in a letter dated 27 June 1888) that "Now, it does not seem to us that the instrument is the primordial object. Sometimes with a poor one great works can be produced; let the Philippine bolo speak. Sometimes in poor literature great truths can be said"

(1999, 96). The allusion to the native "bolo" speaks volumes in the context of pacific writing. It summons the ghosts of women-warriors, from Gabriela Silang, Gregoria de Jesus, Teresa Magbanua, Maria Lorena Barros, Maria Theresa Dayrit, Luisa Dominado-Posa, and countless others.

Without discriminating against other means, Rizal's strategy for the radical transformation of society was neither puritanical nor adventurist. But political agency implied sophistication in ideology-critique. For him, it was not the quality of *belle lettre,* nor aesthetic education alone, that would enable the masses to discover truth and unleash the energies for deliverance. It depended on a fortuitous conjuncture of circumstances, of objective and subjective forces. It involved the "ripeness of time," for the people's spirit blows where it wills. By this time, Rizal was already a marked man. He harbored the stigmata of the *filibustero* avenger, the androgynous shaman haunting the threshold of the temple. Meanwhile Rizal tried to recuperate the lesson of Maria Makiling that he retold in 1890, working under the intractable specters of Sisa, Juli, Dona Consolacion, Dona Victorina, and the ill-fated Maria Clara. Approximating an allegory of a Filipino Monte Cristo, *El Filibusterismo* was published in 1891, shortly after the Boustead affair and his withdrawal from active participation in reformist propaganda in Madrid. In 1892, he was banished to Dapitan. In less than four years, Rizal was dead.

What then is the point of this whole exercise in re-interpreting Rizal in a time of globalized terror and the "shock doctrine" of moribund finance-capitalism? What are the stakes in re-reading Rizal?

A contemporary of Rizal, the American "backwoodsman" Charles Sanders Peirce (1839-1914), the inventor of pragmaticism and arguably the greatest philosopher of modern times, may offer us a justification. A close friend of Harvard sage William James, one of the militant founders of the Anti-Imperialist League, Peirce opposed in his quiet way the ruthless US subjugation of the Philippines in the name of "Manifest Destiny" and a white-supremacist "civilizing mission." He was not as vocal as his New England colleagues, nor as irrepressible as the astute Mark Twain with his scathing diatribes against the US empire (Zwick 1992). Nonetheless, Peirce expressed his deeply felt sympathy for the beleaguered revolutionaries in the course of his fourth Harvard Lecture on "The Seven Systems of Metaphysics," delivered on 16 April 1903. This was two years after the massacre of fifty-nine American soldiers in Balangiga, Samar, Philippines; and a year after the prolamation by Theodore Roosevelt that the war in the Philippines was over (Miller 1982).

Peirce did not believe that the Filipinos had been completely subdued. He believed in the legitimacy of the Filipinos' right to fight for self-determination, as witness the Tagala on the shore appropriating a link, found by accident and transmitted to others; this story alludes to an informing telos in the chain of signifiers that when translated by the community was bound to reinvigorate the resistance against the imperial colossus. Signs produce effects and actualize purposes. Peirce's hidden message of solidarity suddenly materializes in the middle of a discourse on "Thirdness" and on the power of words to generate incalculable effects, an integral part of Peirce's seminal theory of signs. Didn't Rizal, the cunning propagandist and polymath, cherish the belief that his words were bound to produce disturbance and changes of habits in whoever reads/hears them? That may explain for us the rationale for what we have accomplished here, whose value remains to be acknowledged, weighed and tested in practice by the masses for it to become a weapon in the struggle:

...Nobody can deny that words do produce such effects. Take for example, that sentence of Patrick Henry which, at the time of our revolution, was repeated by every man to his neighbor: "Three millions of people, armed in the holy cause of Liberty, and in such a country as we possess, are invincible against any force that the enemy can bring against us."

Those words present this character of the general law of nature, that they might have produced effects indefinitely transcending any that circumstances allowed them to produce. It might, for example. have happened that some American schoolboy, sailing as a passenger in the Pacific Ocean, should have idly written down those words on a slip of paper. The paper might have been tossed overboard and might have been picked up by some Tagala on a beach of the island of Luzon; and if he had them translated to him they might easily have passed from mouth to mouth there as they did in this country, and with similar effect.

Words then do produce physical effects. It is madness to deny it. The very denial of it involves a belief in it; and nobody can consistently fail to acknowledge it until he sinks to a complete mental paresis (1998, 184).

RIZAL AND REVOLUTION IN THE AGE OF IMPERIAL TERRORISM

*Yo la tengo, y yo espero que ha de brillar un dia
en que venza la Idea a la fuerza brutal,
que despues de la lucha y la lenta agonia,
otra vzx mas sonora, mas feliz que la mi
sabra cantar entonces el cantico triunfal.*

[I have the hope that the day will dawn/when the Idea will conquer brutal force; that after the struggle and the lingering travail,/another voice, more sonorous, happier than mine shall know then how to sing the triumphant hymn.]

-- Jose Rizal, "Mi Retiro" (22 October 1895)

On June 19, 2011, we are celebrating 150 years of Rizal's achievement and its enduring significance in this new millennium. It seems fortuitous that Rizal's date of birth would fall just six days after the celebration of Philippine Independence Day - the proclamation of independence from Spanish rule by General Emilio Aguinaldo in Kawit, Cavite, in 1898. In 1962 then President Diosdado Macapagal decreed the change of date from July 4 to June 12 to reaffirm the primacy of the Filipinos' right to national self-determination. After more than three generations, we are a people still in quest of the right, instruments, and opportunity to determine ourselves as an autonomous, sovereign and singular nation-state.

Either ironical or prescient, Aguinaldo's proclamation (read in the context of US Special Forces engaged today in fighting Filipino socialists and other progressive elements) contains the kernel of the contradictions that have plagued the ruling elite's claim to political legitimacy: he invoked the mythical benevolence of the occupying power. Aguinaldo unwittingly mortgaged his leadership to the "protection of the Mighty and Humane North American Nation." Mighty, yes, but "humane"? The U.S. genocide of 1.4 million Filipinos is, despite incontrovertible evidence, still disputed by apologists of "Manifest Destiny." But there is no doubt that Aguinaldo's gratitude to the Americans who brought him back from exile after the Pact of Biak-na-Bato spelled the doom of the *ilustrado* oligarchy which, despite the demagogic ruses of Marcos and his successors, has proved utterly bankrupt in its incorrigible corruption, electoral cynicism, and para-military gangster violence. Obedient to US dictates, the current regime appears to follow its predecessors along the path of neocolonial decadence and barbarism, further opening the country's dwindling resources to predatory transnational corporations and their mercenaries. And so, *sotto voce*: "Long live Filipino Independence Day!"

The 150th anniversary of Rizal's birth affords us the occasion to reassess his work, particularly in the context of ongoing fierce class war between the exploited, impoverished majority and the few privileged landlords, bureaucrats and business moguls patronized by global capital. This is taking place at a time when the Philippines is being re-colonized by the United States, the world's moribund hegemon, under the cover of the global war on terrorism, also labeled Islamic "extremism." The Abu Sayyaf and the New People's Army serve as pretexts for perennial US military intervention. Would Rizal want the country partitioned by greedy corporate speculators and their agents in the ongoing genocidal war against peoples of color?

Numerous biographies celebrate Rizal as "the first Filipino" (Guerrero) "the pride of the Malay Race" (Palma}, even the antithetical American-made hero (Constantino)—the canonical icon of the patriot-liberator (Bonoan 1996) worshipped every June and December. Unless we want to be pharisaical acolytes and hagiographers, we need to renew our commitment to Rizal's ideas, not his image. The commentaries in my previous book *Rizal In Our Time* (1977), as well as my reflections on Rizal's travels in the US (included in *Balikbayang Sinta: An E. San Juan Reader* (2008), seek to provoke a re-thinking of what it means to be a Filipino particularly at a time when the country is undergoing dire, almost perpetual crisis. My essays use Rizal as a catalyzing point of departure, especially in the light of its citizens becoming an embattled diaspora--more than ten million overseas Filipinos (migrants, expatriates) labor as exploited domestics and contract workers scattered around the planet, while their homeland's natural endowments, cultures and traditions are wasted by foreign profiteers supported by comprador parasites who claim to be the elected stewards of the land.

While visiting Cuba in the 1980s, I found millions of Cubans spellbound by Rizal's two novels—read in the original Spanish by more people in Cuba than in the Philippines, or elsewhere. While Rizal did not reach Cuba as a volunteer doctor in 1896, his novels arrived there a hundred years after, thanks to Fidel Castro's and Che Guevara's anti-imperialist revolution (Martinez Ramirez 1961). Rizal as an exile within his own country and as a scholar/traveler in the US and Europe may provide lessons for us in our postmodern but neocolonial deracination. It may yield clues and signposts useful for re-discovering our rich historical tradition of resistance against colonial domination, and our untapped resources for renewing the revolutionary legacy and internationalist solidarity that Rizal embodied in his life and works.

Prologue to an Inquest

Ever since the Renaissance and the rise of the European bourgeoisie, the focus of critical attention has shifted from the cosmic totality to the individual. This individualist metaphysic acquired logical form in Descartes' abolition of doubt by the ego-centered consciousness. The solitary individual, Robinson Crusoe as master-narrative hero, occupied center-stage in mapping the heterogeneous process of worldwide social development. Its culmination in Locke's empiricism and Hegel's idealism reinforced the triumph of the property-owner, the profit-obsessed slave-trader and manufacturer, and eventually the broker-financier of empire. All events and changes in society were ascribed to individual thoughts and private decisions, marginalizing its larger context in the changes in social relations locally and

globally, triggered by profound alterations in the mode of production and reproduction of material life.
Historians followed suit in analyzing the turn of events in their surroundings. By describing heroes and their lives, thinkers believed that they have explained and charted the vicissitudes of whole social domains—until Marx (in "Critique of Hegel's Doctrine of the State" and *The German Ideology*) restored balance by re-locating individual protagonists in the political economy they inhabit.

In the "Theses on Feuerbach," Marx posited that the "human essence is no abstraction inherent in each single individual. In its reality it is the ensemble of the social relations" (1975, 423). In the ultimate analysis, the individual subject may be viewed as a microcosm of the whole social fabric that generates his potential and his actuality, without which this monadic figure has no meaning or consequence. Reciprocally, the opaque density of the social background is illumined and concretely defined by individual acts of intervention, such as Rizal's novels, without which society and the physical world remain indifferent. We need this dialectical approach to comprehend in a more all-encompassing way Rizal's vexed and vexing situation, together with his painstakingly calculated responses—all cunning ruses of Reason in history (for Hegel). Such ruses actually register the contradictions of social forces in real life, reflected in the crises of lives in each generation.

The substantial biographies of Rizal--from Austin Craig to Rafael Palma, Leon Maria Guerrero to Austin Coates--all attempted to triangulate the ideas of the hero with his varying positions in his family, in the circle of his friends and colleagues in Europe, and in relation to the colonial Establishment. Their main concern is to find out the origin of the hero's thoughts and their impact on the local environment. But the twin errors of contemplative objectivism and individualist bias persisted in vitiating their accounts. They ignored the historical-materialist axiom that the changing of circumstances and of personal sensibility/minds, as Marx advised, "can be conceived and rationally understood only as revolutionary practice"—that is, sensuous collective praxis in material life. In Palma's biography, for example, the novelty of Rizal's project of the *Liga Filipina* became simply "a means to defray the expenses of the colonization of Borneo" (1949, 202; see Zaide and Zaide 1984). In reality, the *Liga* is the chief emblematic index of that transformative praxis fusing personal experience and objective circumstances. It is the crucible marking the failure of *La Solidaridad* reformism and the transition to the stage of popular mobilization mediated by the rising organic intellectuals of the dispossessed, in particular Andres Bonifacio, Jacinto, and others. Rizal's radicalizing agenda was already distilled in his bold testimony of communicative action, the eloquent "Letter to the Women of Malolos" (more later), and articulated in the two letters dated June 20, 1892, letters whose resonance and value can perhaps be compared only to St. Paul's epistles to the early converts of the faith.

By all accounts, the formation of the *Liga* is the key event marking Rizal's leap from intellectual gradualism to collective separatism. Before his exile to Dapitan in 1892, Rizal met with members of the Masonic Balagtas Lodge in the home of Doroteo Onjungco, including Ambrosio Salvador, Timoteo Paez, Pedro Serrano, Domingo Franco, and, last but not least, Andres Bonifacio, who was then not distinguishable from the crowd of about thirty individuals. After Governor Despujol decreed Rizal's banishment, the *Liga* members met secretly in the Azcarraga apartment of Deodato Arellano, among them Andres Bonifacio and Gregorio Del Pilar, who later died fighting American troops pursuing the fleeing Aguinaldo headed for Palanan (Palma 1949, 225). That historic gathering of seven persons signaled the launching of the *Katipunan,* the organization of "sons of the people" committed to overthrowing Spanish colonial tyranny.

Coincidentally, then, the banishment of Rizal to the southern outpost of Dapitan occurred with the implementation of decisions to liberate the country from the stranglehold of the "mother country," Spain. That sequence of events at this conjuncture of Rizal's life, as

Floro Quibuyen (1999) and others have shown, epitomizes the translation of ideas into organized mass activism, a description of the political shift that is less problematic than the reappropriation of the *pasyon* by popular consciousness (Ileto 1998). Spontaneous mass strikes and actions are blind, ineffectual and self-defeating without the mediation of organic intellectuals and organized leadership, as Rizal's contemporaries Bakunin and Kropotkin (Laqueur 1978; Guerin 1970) have argued. *Rizal's Fili* is a cogent demonstration of that truth.

Critique of the Orthodox Canon

So far we have sketched in this book a historical-materialist approach to Rizal's thought and career. Its foundational premise is that Rizal is a social and historical product of his time, actor and acted upon in specific historical circumstances. We know that Rizal blamed fate on the eve of his execution, but he did not disavow responsibility for acts that led to that denouement. He was not a tragic hero, simply a combatant spokesman of all the subjugated in the anti-colonial war. He incarnated the critical universality of the Philippine revolution. While Rizal was formed by his sociopolitical milieu, he interacted with specific actors/players and tried to synthesize the disparate forces and convergent tendencies in his unique situation. To separate the psyche from the historical situation would result in the flamboyant psychologizing of Ante Radaic and other postmodernist gurus; conversely, to ignore Rizal's concrete life-situation is to simplify and reify the pressures of his dynamic milieu.

One would expect Leon Maria Guerrero to be more nuanced and circumspect. In his magisterial biography, however, the endeavor to explain Rizal as a phenomenon of his time dissolves into untenable speculations. Following Cesar Majul's reading of Rizal's concept of a Filipino national community supplanting the traditional assemblage of creoles and subaltern natives under the Spanish Crown and the Roman Catholic Church, Guerrero jumps to the conclusion that the *Liga* presumed the unity of all classes, entirely unlike Bonifacio's Katipunan.

Consequently, opposed to Rizal's dialectical synthesis of thought and action in oppositional praxis, Guerrero continues the mechanical disjunction of unity, and then prosperity for all natives first before independence, a proposition he attributes to Rizal (1969, 429). Guerrero reads the exchanges between Ibarra and Elias in the *Noli* with the same moralizing drive, while the dialogue between Simoun and Basilio in the *Fili* is interpreted as a symptom of Rizal's disillusionment with Spain. But Simoun's plan of exacerbating abuses, sowing mayhen, inciting crowds to revolt—the telltale anarchist syndrome--is rejected in Father Florentino's sermon. The priest avers that "the sword no longer wields much influence on the destinies of our age" and that "our sufferings are our own fault." Guerrero congeals the tension of clashing beliefs, making Rizal a partisan of the evolutionist party rather than grasping the dynamic realism (immanent in the Ibarra/Simoun double) of calculating ends and means in accordance with the volatile, ceaselessly mutating level of the spontaneous political impulse of the masses and the initiatives of their organic leaders. The Rizal *problematique* escapes such a paralyzing maneuver.

Arguing the thesis that Rizal is a reluctant revolutionary, Guerrero cannot avoid a dualistic, either/or viewpoint which privileges selected episodes/ideas of the hero's career. He contends that the *Liga* was designed only for recruiting rich progressives and liberal intellectuals—we saw Bonifacio and other plebeian activists present during its inaugural moments--while the Katipunan was intended mainly to attract the proletarian horde. Guerrero's static and economistic prejudice infects his whole biography, as obvious in the prolix sophistry of his discourse so reminiscent of Cold War polemics in the aftermath of World War II. Here is a specimen of Guerrero's pontifications:

But any difference in their social objectives was undefined and unspoken; Rizal read Voltaire and Bonifacio read Carlyle and the "Lives of the American Presidents"; neither seems to have read Marx or Bakunin or Proudhon. Both the Liga and the Katipunan, therefore, were based on the comfortable theory of the social compact: unity, mutual protection and mutual help. But neither was aware of the issue that was already tearing western civilization apart: the choice between liberty and equality (1969, 431).

Can anyone take seriously this tendentious disjunction between liberty and equality as anything but a disguised re-statement of the ideological conflict between the pseudo-liberty of capitalist business society and the postulated equality of atheistic communism? Liberty of an exclusive few without equality is what Rizal condemned and struggled against, precisely that ruthless autocratic behemoth (Spain's decadent empire) to which Elias' ancestors, Sisa's children, and Cabesang Tales' family were sacrificed. In a world of widespread poverty, official criminality, and imperial wars in the 1950s and 1960s, especially the brutal campaign against the Huks, liberty for whom? Liberty for what?

Of course, one cannot fault Guerrero for being a product of his own milieu. Just as one cannot criticize Nick Joaquin for being a diehard apologist for the *ilustrado* generation of surviving creoles (from Fr. Jose Burgos to Trinidad Pardo de Tavera) and their descendants whose passing he laments. Joaquin's total oeuvre is a melodramatic elegy to its demise. In his two essays on Rizal in *A Question of Heroes,* Joaquin compares and contrasts Guerrero and Radaic's portraits of Rizal. He praises Guerrero's crafted narrative of Rizal's career as a kind of "anti-hero." Guerrero argues that the 1896 revolution was hatched in Spain by the propertied bourgeoisie to which Rizal and the *propagandistas* belonged. Guerrero believes that Rizal's retraction (his disavowal of Masonic and rationalist errors) was authentic; that Rizal's apostolate did not give him real social consciousness and so he remained a member of the petit-bourgeois intelligentsia. Rizal's nationalism was "essentially rationalist," anti-clerical and anti-racist, political rather than social or economic. In short, Rizal was the typical Victorian sage who believed in the dogma of reason, inevitable progress through science and commerce, and the efficacy of parliamentary representation, even up to the last moments of his life.

Rizal was an evolutionist or eventualist politician, not a revolutionary intellectual.

Lest he be accused of partiality, Guerrero acknowledges the ambivalences in Rizal's writings, if not in his varying standpoints at different stages of his life. Cognizant of his privileged background, Rizal sympathized with the oppressed and exploited, with Sisa's family and Cabesang Tales' clan. We recall how his family and relatives suffered enormously when they were ejected from their homes by the Dominican friars in October-November 1981. But, according to Guerrero, Rizal was afraid of the "bloody apparitions" of violence, the excesses of "premature conspiracies," especially those committed by the mobs of yesterday's slaves become today's tyrants—to echo Father Florentino's glib dismissal of *filibusteros*. Guerrero could not disregard this, so he begrudgingly calls Rizal a "reluctant revolutionary" who condemned the means used by Bonifacio but not the aim of overthrowing the colonial power. Rizal suffered from a Hamlet-like schizophrenia, his will to act paralyzed by scruples and reservations—a trait acutely observed by Miguel de Unamuno, but blown to disproportionate importance by Radaic in his psychoanalytic diagnosis of Rizal as a "delicate human problem." Rizal may have united both subversive and progressive elements, but he did not create the idea of the nation on his own and so became the "first Filipino," as Joaquin notes in his chronicling of the irreconcilable hostility between the creoles and the peninsulares.

Purging the Sins of the Fathers

Both Guerrero and Joaquin seem to share the notion that before Spain's arrival, the Philippines was comprised of separate, disjoined, non-communicating primitive tribes. At best, the numerous revolts of Dagohoy, Malong, Almazen, Hermano Pule, and others later called "cultural minorities" signified mere ethnic group demands, parochial and detached from each other. For Joaquin, it was Spain and Christianity that molded the diverse tribes into one. Joaquin declares that Spanish colonial rule served as the matrix or womb that enabled

Rizal and other creole ilustrados to envision a compact and homogeneous society based on common interests and mutual protection rather than allegiance to Spain and the Catholic Church. At the same time, however, it could not escape the notice of our two apologists that all those revolts, removed from each other in time and space, in one degree or another share an origin in common grievances and fate: the abuses of the institutional power of Church and State. It was this oppressive feudal/tributary relation of production, founded on the monopoly of productive means by the colonizing power, which generated collective protests and insurrections periodically, throughout the islands. Meanwhile, the Igorots, Moros and other pagan communities resisted and could not be subdued by Spanish might, utilizing various native groups conscripted into the military apparatus. They are lumped together with bandits, outlaws, and pariahs as inhuman "others" close to the animal kingdom and so could be destroyed any time with impunity.

Owing to various changes in the mode of production from Legaspi's time to the eighteenth century, a small merchant-farming class of creoles arose in the nineteenth century from which Rizal and other *ilustrados* emerged. It was not a bourgeoisie according to the European model, but a petty bourgeoisie of creoles/mestizos (Spanish, Chinese, Indios intermarrying) composed of small farmers, merchants, artisans, and their educated children that sprang from the interstices of the colonial structure. Through the institutions of highly regulated schools, printing press, and secular business, this group flourished intermittently until it came into direct conflict with Spanish civil and religious authority that then gradually lost its legitimacy in failing to take into account the growing material wealth and power of this new group of *principales*. In time, the ideology and principles of this emergent sector constituted a counterhegemonic bloc that Rizal allied himself with.

The secularization movement among the clergy initially spearheaded by creoles (witness the martyred priests Jose Burgos, Mariano Gomez, and Jacinto Zamora) was the culmination of the upheaval in the economic and political infrastructures. Its impact can be discerned both in the *ilustrado* demand for reforms and in the hardening reactionary defensiveness of the religious orders and the weak or indifferent Spanish officials representing the Madrid government. Obscurantist dogmatism and feudal authoritarian practices, from 1972 to the outbreak of the 1896 insurrection, could no longer plausibly claim to represent the talent, money, aspirations and other interests of the creoles. Joaquin argues that from the 1820 Novales revolt to the 1840 Palmares conspiracy, up to the secularizing agitation led by Father Pelaez in the 1850-60s, this creole movement paralleled the mobilization of its Latin American counterparts Bolivar, San Martin, and others, which eventually liberated the continent from Spanish control. This is the reason Rizal's hero, Juan Crisostomo Ibarra, was a creole descended from Basque ancestors, gentlemen landowners, who had become naturalized, as it were, in the colony. Like Rizal (though more Chinese than Spanish), Ibarra was thus a "translated Filipino," not a primordial Indio or Malay indigene.

From this historical vantage point, Joaquin belabors his argument to dovetail with Guerrero's opinion that Rizal was "the first Filipino." He was "first" only in the sense that Rizal vigorously articulated in his essays, particularly in his annotations on Morga's chronicle and in "The Philippines A Century Hence," the imperative of solidarity among the aboriginal ethnolinguistic groups inhabiting the islands in the face of an illegitimate occupying power. It is not clear if Rizal would include the Moros and other Lumads into this assemblage of rational literate constituencies. In any case, it goes against the grain of facts and public consensus to insist that Hispanization in the 19th century was proceeding well after the victories against competing European powers that finally broke the siege mentality of Intramuros. And it is rather special pleading to argue that despite the abuses of the friars and corrupt officials, the centuries-long resistance to Dutch and British invaders (with their schismatic Protestantism) involving creoles and native soldiers from Pampanga, Ilocos and the Tagalog regions who allegedly were not mercenaries, can be considered the narrative of the making of the Filipino nation. Whatever the subtle discriminations in their discourse, for Joaquin and Guerrero, the Spanish-descended creoles and their Indio subalterns constituted the Filipino nation long before the rise of the Katipunan and the establishment of the short-lived Malolos Republic. And so the millions of Indios who were forced to work in the mines, build the galleons, and sacrifice their lives in the military campaigns to suppress the local revolts were all complicit in the genesis of the Filipino as a distinct national formation. Would Rizal's eventualism and even self-righteous horror at the "highly absurd" Katipunan uprising support such a genealogical hypothesis? Could this lesson in nation-making be part of the Malolos women's curriculum and self-administered tutelage?

Joaquin finally argues that the Rizal phenomenon encapsulates the vicissitudes of the creole anti-Spanish insurrection from the 1870s (the Cavite Mutiny and execution of the three priests) to the 1890s (the termination of *La Solidaridad* and the abortive founding of the *Liga Filipina*). As Rizal himself said, he became a radical because of the failure of Pelaez-Burgos' peaceful secularization campaign. This is the logic behind the transition from the naïve reformism of the *Noli* to the proto-anarchist, more precisely adventurist, play of ideas and character dispositions in the *Fili*. While the *Noli* 's outlook is assimilationist in the mode of the liberalizing (not yet libertarian) creoles Rizal admired, the *Fili*'s stance is separatist, following the anti-obscurantist Marcelo del Pilar and the Americanizing T. H. Pardo de Tavera. Rizal's trajectory also mirrors the transition from preoccupation with Morga's records of the past and with "On the Indolence of Filipinos," to the prophetic deliberations of "The Philippines a Century Hence." Time conquers space; history overcomes the fetish of the transcendent. And Aguinaldo trumps Bonifacio, Luna and Mabini.

Anatomy of the Hero's Soul

Readers generally want happy endings. The scholastic prejudice is that Rizal summarized his whole life in the sermon of Padre Florentino at the end of the *Fili*, particularly in the now worn-out slogan: "To suffer and to work!" But this is precisely what Cabesang Tales, Basilio, Isagani, and others did, all to no avail. Evil was not diminished, much less extinguished; God remained hidden, eclipsed, "disappeared, " and finally neutralized, with the victims dismissed as "collateral damage" (to use the Pentagon parlance). Justice delays, procrastinates, malingers somewhere. On the other hand, we should not ignore the ambiguity of the priest's counsel, which implies that work—collective praxis engaged by the bondsmen and colonized subalterns—transforms character and collective destiny. After alleging that force no longer plays a role in the shaping of modern polities, Padre Florentino continues: "...yes, but we must win it [freedom] , deserving it, raising the intelligence and the dignity of the individual, loving the just, the good, the great, even dying for it, and when a people reach that height, God provides the weapon, and the idols fall, the tyrants fall like a house of cards and liberty shines with the first dawn" (2004, 410).

From Rizal's deistic optic, "God" here is a shorthand term for "history" epitomized in the eschatological turn of events. God's presence is ascertainable from the classic saying: "*vox populi vox dei.*" Padre Florentino does not hedge his bets in the agnostic, millenarian wager: both passive empiricism (suffer) and active engagement (work) constitute the unfolding of human capabilities in the development of human knowledge and scientific control and manipulation of nature's forces. Rizal's faith in rational self-regulation and technological progress may be perceived even in Padre Florentino's belief that time and nature are on the side of the just; after throwing Simoun's wealth to the ocean, he exclaims: "May Nature guard you in her deep abysses among the corals and pearls of her eternal seas!...When for a holy and sublime end men should need you, God will draw you from the breast of the waves..." (2004, 413). Human necessity becomes God's accomplice; fatalism is thus circumvented. But we know that it is merely a token gesture, for the social wealth that unequally circulates in the world continues to distort right and foment avarice, contrary to the cleric's fanciful wish-fulfillment. Subjective will power cannot transcend by its own efforts the limitations of objective social reality.

This is the ambition of psychologically-oriented critics such as Ante Radaic (1999) and other biographers concentrating on idiosyncratic aspects of Rizal's personality. From the Victorian anti-hero of Guerrero, we move to the psychoanalytic case study of Radaic, the modern man afflicted with existential anguish. Radaic's theory of Rizal's character is simple: Rizal's physical inadequacies—short height, frail or puny body, etc.—produced an inferiority complex that drove him to compensate by cultivating his intellectual resources and sharpening his skills in artistic endeavors (writing, musical and theatrical performances, amorous games, etc.). Rizal's physical defects, heightened by an introjected ideal image of the body, the ideal "I" or ego, generated a discordance or imbalance that needed correction. According to Radaic, the symptom for this unresolved predicament may be seen in a spiritual excess that manifested itself in extreme scrupulosity, indecisiveness, melancholy, and terror of certain unknown forces outside the tranquility of home in Calamba and the protection of his mother and father. In other words, the diminutive size of Rizal's body explains both positive and negative aspects of his life: his omnivorous capacity in learning languages, his inexhaustible intellectual curiosity, his prolific writing, restless amorous engagements, and so on. But did Rizal's activities resolve the contradiction between appearance and reality, reason and irrationality?

So we confront a "deep and delicate human problem" personified by Rizal. His exile and travels symbolize this problem of discrepancy between the interior and exterior, between his ideals and his constrained situation. The result is recorded in a nostalgia-laden confession found in *Memorias de Un Estudiante* to which we have already alluded in previous chapters: "At the critical moments of my life I have always acted against my will, obeying other ends and powerful duties." Unamuno, Retana and others have commented on this typical dilemma: the bold dreamer with a weak will, irresolute in action, withdrawing and delaying ("filibustering" may be the appropriate epithet, though the Spanish "filibusterismo" has more subversive, sinister connotations), terrified by the "bloody apparitions" of political turbulence. This has also engendered the thought of a "multitudinous"Rizal, a character with miraculous protean qualities, easily switching positions—from reformist to revolutionary, and back—difficult to pin down. He also tended to view sexual love as a "yoke" that can imprison, a constricting burden. Radaic thinks this is a symptom of sexual inadequacy, whether real or imagined, as shown in his attitude toward Segunda Katigbak. Rizal's pathogenic and neurotic personality harbors wounds that refuse to heal, driving him to compensate by channeling frustrated energies to other activities, sublimating libidinal impulses by other means. In other words, his whole life may be seen as an attempt to ascend from his self-perceived physical deformity to superior heights.

Surely there were millions suffering from those defects in the nineteenth century, but none of them approximates the historical figure of Rizal. Sartre once said that Paul Valery is a bourgeois poet, but not all members of the bourgeois class can be considered Valery. In short, determing the class identity and clan/racial lineage of an individual, much less his physical dimensions, does not provide any clue toward adequately explaining the historically specific social phenomenon called "Rizal." The same applies to Radaic's version of the Rizal complex: not only is it reductive and distorting, it also endorses a toxic ideology of individualism that Rizal himself repudiated at various crises of his life. His monumental sacrifices to complete his novels, as well as his efforts to rescue his family from privations, and other acts of sympathy and solidarity with others, are incontestable proofs. Moreover, the putative "individualism" of colonial subjects in 19th-century Philippines is a peculiar morbidity that cannot be mistaken for the neurotic individualism of modern industrial society.

Alienation in an obsolescent Spanish colony cannot be equated to anomie and reification in twentieth-century Europe or North America. Since others have spent time and energy demonstrating the limits of the doctrinaire psychoanalytic treatment applied to Rizal, I would suggest to adventurous inquirers to re-appraise Rizal's life from a historical-materialist standpoint. They should foreground those writings in which he disavowed this fallacy of self-serving, mendacious individualism as a method of understanding the complexity of the human condition traversed and contoured by diverse historical contingencies.

Either/Or: Hermeneutics of Suspects

The debate on Rizal's contemporary significance pivots around the issue of whether Rizal was an authentic revolutionary, or a mere American idol foisted on naïve subalterns. To put it in Renato Constantino's dichotomizing option, the choice is whether we should follow Rizal or Bonifacio as the modern national hero (1970, 125-46; see Ocampo 1998). It's a wager for high stakes. On occasion, Rizal himself entertained a moralistic dualism when he asserts in "Cuento Tendencioso," for instance: "*Ang sagot sa dahas ay dahas, kapag bingi sa katuwiran*" {The response to force is force, if the other is deaf to reason]. To be sure, Rizal parodied the moralizing opportunism of his contemporaries in satires such as "By Telephone," "The Vision of Fr. Rodriguez," and "Reflections of a Filipino" (1974). Antinomies of thought cannot be solved by abstract casuistry, divorced from the concrete historical specificities, the determinant limits and possibilities of each situation.

No doubt Rizal wanted a total reconstruction of society, a wide-ranging and thoroughgoing transformation. But how? By whom? With what? While the genealogy of Rizal's concept of the nation—the core of Rizal's moral realism that postcolonial critics reject as monistic, totalizing, linear, homogenizing, etc.—in Enlightenment humanism and universal altruism is no longer a point of controversy, the question of Rizal's praxis remains highly contentious. That praxis, based on popular education and the exercise of civic virtues, is premised on the self-development of an inborn potential, the species being of *homo sapiens* (for the American canonization of Rizal, see Kramer 2006; one anti-imperialist eulogy is exemplified by Bigelow 1899). Nonetheless, the bureaucrats continue to sanctify the conventional iconic Rizal, ignoring the Rizal of the 1892 letters, the letter to the Malolos women, among other writings, and the aborted project of the *Liga* and its call to Filipinos to assume responsibility—that is, to exercise their freedom by criticizing and subverting the oppressive, irrational order.

Rizal is the prophet of an Enlightenment philosophy founded on the imperative of humans overthrowing the gods and claiming their worldly freedom. This Promethean vocation is still formulated in scholastic terms. Four years before his death, he wrote to Father Pastells while in exile in Dapitan: "...but I rejoice more when I contemplate humanity in its immortal march, always progressing in spite of its declines and falls, in spite of its aberrations, because that demonstrates to me its glorious end and tells me that it has been created for a better purpose than to be consumed by flames; it fills me with trust in God, who will not let His work be ruined, in spite of the devil and of all our follies" (dated Nov. 11, 1892). But this evolutionist creed was counterpointed by chiliastic interruptions and millenarian impulses, as evinced not only in the novels but also in his letters and essays. However, the metaphysical disposition of idealizing thought separate from social practice persists. Skeptical individualism intrudes in the guise of a salvific messiah. This is why we choose to highlight and valorize aspects of Rizal's highly adaptive, versatile, conjunctural thinking relative to our own purposes regardless of their determinant contexts and their entanglement in particular circumstances. In short, we fashion the Rizal we want to revere, disregarding the totality of his life and the milieu that circumscribe the serviceability and pragmatic import of his ideas. We invent our own Rizal, afraid to confront the challenge of self-contradictory reality and act on it.

But before this program of re-invention becomes exorbitant and self-serving, let us for a moment reflect on what inspires it. In the light of Benedict Anderson's fascinating book *Under Three Flags* (2005), which deals more with the influence of anarchism in Europe, Asia and Latin America rather than with Rizal or Filipino nationalism *per se*, it would be timely to re-open the issue of Rizal's equivocations. I fully agree with Jim Richardson's (2006) shrewd and incisive comments on Anderson's errors and limitations. One notable failure of intelligence is Anderson's judgment that Rizal was really not "a political thinker," but merely a moralist and novelist. Anderson set out to chart the gravitational force of selected anarchist ideas—not so much the classic versions of Proudhon and Bakunin but of the propagandist of deeds (bomb throwing, assassinations, terror) extolled by Errico Malatesta, Sergey Nechayev, Fernando Tarrida del Marmol, and others. In the process of deploying montage, serialized and episodic narration spiced with a gratuituous sprinkling of Eurocentric hauteur, Anderson only achieves what Richardson calls an "illusion of interconnectedness." Anderson's "political astronomy" could not identify correctly the shifting valence and the gravitational force of the myriad constellations in the galaxy of traveling anarchism. For example, Anderson considers the *Fili* incoherent, acerbic toward liberals but lax toward the lecherous friars, "largely oblivious or indifferent to the social misery in Europe itself" (2005, 108), and its hero Simoun nothing but a "cynical nihilist conspirator." Simoun's malady is traced to "an unscrupulous and cruel Basque grandfather" and the failed conspiracy a poor imitation of European ones, such as the 1892 Jerez uprising and those of the assassins Ravachol and Auguste Vaillant.

Anderson's treatise strives to delineate the a*narchisant*, not anarchist, temper of Rizal's *Fili*. The presumably cynical, nihilist Simoun had no solid plan after the success of his revenge, only a dream of a formless, utopian liberty, hence its failure. Anderson's conclusion recapitulates his thematic intent of classifying Rizal as a minor constellation in the galaxy of global anarchism:

It is exactly here that Rizal marked the crisscrossing of anticolonial nationalism and "propaganda by the deed," with its planless utopianism and its taste for self-immolation. From my deed and death something will come which will be better than the unlivable present.... [Simoun] is a sort of *espectro mundial* come to haunt the Philippines, mirroring what Izquierdo had once fantasized as the invisible machiavellian network of he International. Not there yet in reality, but, since already imagined, just like his nation, on the way.... ...Europe itself, Rizal thought, was menaced by a vast conflagration among its warring powers, but also by violent movement from below (2005, 121).

Overall, the *Fili* then is not so much a realistic depiction of events in the Philippines but a premonitory if not prophetic unfolding of what's to come. It functions as a seismograph of the tremulous, convulsive, phantasmagoric future looming on the horizon—the revolt of the Katipunan's unwashed masses, and soon after the invasion of the Yankee troops complete with their sophisticated "water cure," scorched-earth hamletting, and summary executions of village folk. Gramsci's insight fits nicely this anticipated in-between, transitional phase: "The old is dying and the new cannot be born; in this interregnum there arises a great variety of morbid symptoms." Isagani's enigmatic smile and regret at having averted the cataclysm may be diagnosed as one of these multifarious symptoms, and Padre Florentino's work-and-suffer nostrum as another.

An Inventory of Symptoms

There seems to be no clear proof that Rizal sympathized with or held anarchist convictions. But it is impossible to believe that throughout his sojourn in Europe he was insulated from the ideas of Proudhon, Bakunin, Kropotkin, and others. It was part of the cultural climate, the atmosphere of intellectual conversations. He was probably acquainted with the socialist inclination of his contemporaries Juan Luna, Mariano Ponce, Teodoro Sandiko, and others. Rizal might not have conversed with the two Russian nihilists in the drawing room of his friend Pardo de Tavera in Paris in the 1880s, he was probably aware of reports about Russian scientific and cultural developments. As a revealing clue to Rizal's wide internationalist contacts in Madrid alone, not to mention during his travels, note the roster of distinguished guests at the 1884 banquet in honor of Juan Luna and Felix Resurrecion Hidalgo at which Rizal was the main speaker (Baron-Fernandez 1980, 74-76)—a landmark even for the propagandistas.

But never mind, Richardson counsels us, the rhizomal network of anarchism might have penetrated into the interstices of Rizal's psyche, as suggested by certain leitmotifs caught in discourse, grammatology, and the ambiguities of language. While Rizal affirmed the dignity of the autonomous individual, this did not imply a glorification of self-serving deeds nor an unqualified endorsement of the authority of abstract principles, contrary to what Anderson says of Rizal's intention in founding the Liga. The Constitution of the Liga by itself is not a self-evident performative text detached from the field-force of collective action and institutional practice.

One example of the pomodernist hubris of textualizing everything may be found in the reading of the Fili as a parable of the filibustero as epitome of Otherness, the phantom alien body that discombobulates all static, definitive meanings. This anti-authoritarian figure unsettles hierarchy, all fixed and stable identities. It signifies a power of translation or transmission that crosses boundaries and mixes everything. Vicente Rafael postulates that the slippery role of this outsider/foreigner may be taken as the key to grasping the edgy, nervous, embryonic kind of nationalism:

We can think of the Fili as the site within which [Rizal] rehearsed this ambivalence at the foundation of nationalist sentiments. The novel is a record of the hesitations and anxieties raised by the failure of assimilation, giving rise to the specters of separation. The figure of the filibustero was its medium for tracking and trafficking in the emergence, spread, and containment of such anxieties. It is this fundamentally unsettling nature of the filibustero as both medium and message that infests, as it were, both the author and his characters (2003, 170-71).

In a letter to the Austrian scientist Ferdinand Blumentritt, Rizal confessed that he heard the word "filibustero" for the first time in 1872 when the "tragic executions" of Burgos, Gomez and Zamora occurred: "It does not have the meaning of 'pirate'; it means rather a dangerous patriot who will soon be on the gallows, or else a conceited fellow" (Guerrero 1969, 271). But the novel focuses on the activity or movement of "filibusterism," not on single dissidents such as Simoun or Cabesang Tales. Protagonists are meaningless removed from the constituting narrative structure. Further, the failure of Macaraig and other reformers (assimilationists) does not automatically give rise to Simoun's apocalyptic vision of a whole society's death and renewal. The task of deconstructing an elite-sponsored nationalism, however treacherous and tyrannical, cannot be assigned to the trope of the filibustero precisely because the nascent elite then was suppressed before it could flourish; hence Padre Florentino's extreme unction/consoling speech falls on the defunct ears of the dying subversive.

The Fili was dedicated to the memory of the three priests-martyrs who were implicated, without admissible evidence, with the 1872 Cavite Mutiny. Rizal accused the government of shrouding the martyrs' cause "with mystery and obscurities." Accordingly, his aim in writing the novel is to demystify and expose, as elaborated in his address "to the Filipino People and their Government": "Setting aside, therefore, the old custom of respecting myths in order not to encounter the dreaded reality, we look at it face to face instead of fleeing, and with assertive though inexpert hand, we raise the shroud in order to uncover before the multitude the structure of the skeleton." More exactly, Rizal wanted to display to the multitude the rotting cadaver of colonial society, the repulsive decay of the corporeal scaffold of its skeleton.

Unlike the magician Dr. Leeds, Rizal the novelist seeks to dissolve magical secrets, hypocrisies, abusive practices using sacred trappings and taboos. In the Noli likewise, Rizal aimed to expose the social cancer "on the steps of the temple" (that is, by publication of his truth-bearing testimony) so that each one who would come to invoke the Divine, would propose a cure, implicating himself in this therapeutic scheme: "I will lift part of the shroud that conceals your illness, sacrificing to the truth everything, even my own self-respect, for, as your son, I also suffer in your defects and failings." In exploring the variegated worldviews and mentalities of his characters mapped in varying situations, Rizal engaged in the project of radical social critique.

Indicting Maledictions

The power of Rizal's critique cannot be over-emphasized. One of its basic dimensions consists of exploding the illusion of the inevitability of events by showing that the aura of fatality surrounding them is due to how we conceive them, due to our own frame of mind, attitudes, dispositions (to paraphrase Buck-Morrs [2003, 42]. Rizal's critique of colonial ideology via mimesis and symbolism involves the act of disrupting the colonial-theocratic apparatus of mystification that surrounds the "moment of truth" found in every effort of understanding life and social experience; in turn, this moment of discovery is then subsumed or superseded within a more comprehensive theory of explaining the contradictions between belief and reality, truth and appearance, that bedevils all interpellated subjects in society (for dialectical theory, see Howard 1977).

Inscribed within the general contradiction between colonized exploited native bodies and universal religion preaching the transcendent community of all souls, we find the particular contradiction between the social classes, genders, ethnicities and nationalities in the colony. For Rizal, the species-being, what is potentially human but repressed in Filipinos, is in conflict with the prevailing institutional structures and norms. In this light, Simoun (as well as Tasio and Padre Florentino) refract in themselves not only as individuals but also as members of a community (potential or real), the particular plight of the filibustero, which is a pivotal moment in the dynamic unfolding of self-contradictory social processes in which everyone is embedded. Filibusterismo is the name of this interlinked acts of refraction, suturing and demystification.

Rizal's position then cannot be reduced to that of one character's conduct and pronouncements. His project is exploratory, heuristic, and experimental. An illustration of his heteroglotic or carnivalesque (to borrow Bakhtin's terms) mode of critique—the negative-positive movement of supersession performed by articulating the voices of his characters with their intersecting fates--may be found in the confrontation between Ibarra and Tasio in the *Noli*. We know that Tasio prefigures many other characters in the novel whose ambitions are foiled and hopes thwarted; he remains unreconciled to what exists, on the level of thought and behavior. What is striking is not his nonconformist attitudes but his rebellious prophetic stance. He anticipates Simoun when he responds to Ibarra's declaration of trust in religion and state authority. He also foreshadows Ibarra's fall as he proceeds to acquire and disseminate knowledge of the truth of what's going on:

The people do not complain because they have no voice, do not move because they are lethargic, and you say that they do not suffer, because you have not seen their hearts bleed. But one day you will see and you will hear, and ah! woe unto them that build their strength on ignorance or in fanaticism; woe unto them who are engaged in deception and work in darkness, believing that all are asleep! When the light of day illuminates the monster of the shadows, the terrible reaction will come: so much strength bottled up over centuries; so much venom distilled drop by drop; so much lament suppressed will come out and explode... Who then will square those accounts which the peoples of the world present from time to time and which history preserves for us, etched on bloody pages? (Noli 2004, 226).

Note the thematic synapse comprised of the imagery and rhetoric of concealment, unveiling, the shift from darkness to light, discovery as an explosion, release, and the shock of recognition in receiving the message written on "bloody pages." All these presage the itinerary of events in both novels, particularly Simoun's machination in stirring up the monsters in the shadows, with the bottled wrath boiling over and blasting that scene of reconciliation: the wedding of Paulita Gomez and Juanito Pelaez in Chapter 14 of the *Fili*. The otherwise radical Isagani, with his ideals projected onto the beloved, refuses to abandon the siren of dreams and thus aborts Simoun's plot: the unleashing of reality's contradictions—the positive submerged in the negative—only to succumb to the narcotic inertia of the status quo. In the dialectical spin of events, unmasking fails and succeeds at the same time.

The theme of curing a diseased body politic leads to some surprising twists. If knowledge of truth cannot remedy the split between the universal (God) and the local (suffering, injustice, evil), what can? In my gloss on Rizal's novels, I applied a structuralist frame of analysis revolving around the syntagmatic axis of history articulated with the paradigmatic vector of nature. Somehow, a fatality approximating the natural (Sisa's misfortunes) deflects the trajectory of linear progress. Rizal/Ibarra, our Enlightenment hero, still clings to the hope that God's eclipse, his hidden presence, would end, and that divine intervention would bring back the golden age of justice, equality, the happy reunion of loved ones, prosperity, peace. Like his literary analogue, Alexandre Dumas' Count of Monte Cristo, Simoun, evoking Karamazov's and Job's existential anguish, seeks to resurrect the dead God (before Nietzsche's proclamation) and fulfill the promise of redemption. Critique, pedagogical reconstruction , is Ibarra's way of satisfying that promise. Critique may be also be discerned in Tasio's universalist thinking, which is supplanted in the *Fili* by Padre Florentino's exorcism of Simoun, an attempt to heal the rupture between the profane and sacred by converting Nature/Culture to become the servant of the divine will. All schemes of exchange, transmission and circulation of signs—the signifiers of the past, customs, blood kinship—are displaced by the characteristic move in Rizal to remind us that his allegory speaks to the real and addresses living bodies in the hope of generating changes in actuality. The ripeness of *filibusterismo* is all: resistance, dissidence, revolution

Rizal's moral realism understands the limits and shortcomings of fallible human agency. But it does not give up the vocation of changing society because it is founded on the gap between what exists and what is desired. We have seen the ethico-political motivation of allegorical realism dramatized at the end of Chapter 10 of the *Fili*. After Cabesang Tales stole Simoun's revolver and killed his oppressors, leaving his name "Tales" beside the mutilated body of the usurper's wife, Rizal launches into the famous cry for revenge, for Spain to render justice to the victims: "Do not be alarmed, peaceful citizens of Calamba. Not one of you is called Tales, not one of you has committed the crime....You have served Spain and the King and when in their names you asked for justice and you were exiled without due process of law, you were snatched away from the arms of your spouses, from the kisses of your children...." (*Fili* 97). His appeal is still directed to the authorities, not to the toilers and pariahs. Lest we forget about Sisa's sufferings, Rizal replicates her misfortune in Juli's plight. Meanwhile, we know that Simoun/Ibarra, like the magician/deity operating behind the scenes, no longer believes that "generous Spain" will heed the prayer of the novelist, nor heed the conscience of Padre Florentino. In a world without god (the colonizing leviathan), it is necessary for humans to assume responsibility and decide collectively, in solidarity, their common fate. The theory and practice of freedom by the insurgent people is the essence of moral realism.

Both novels employ the method of allegorical realism to test the hypothesis of human freedom born from insurgent practice, replacing a transcendent power/demiurge as the shaper and arbiter of history. Realism, the style and technique of reproducing the thickness of quotidian life, is harnessed for the purpose of critique. But critique has a double function: to negate but also to salvage what is valuable and reappropriate it into a new enlarged, richer frame of rationality. This integration in Rizal often takes the form of a fantasy sequence that, as soon as summoned and allowed to dance, is mocked. One sequence evaporates only to be immediately supplemented by a new massing of events, raw sensory materials. This process leads to another accumulation of grotesque shapes, excessive rites, contrivances and commodities become fetish confounding the sacred with the profane, magical paraphernalia (as in Dr. Leeds' show in the Quiapo Fair reinforced by other indices such as the crocodile in the lake; the ghost in the roof of the Santa Clara Convent, Simoun's jewelry, and so on). Juxtaposed to the fantastic sequence is the utopian segment often accompanied by the melodramatic atmosphere of scenes and settings haunted by intersecting characters: *filibusteros*, bandits, the dislocated and ostracized, and other stigmatized groups hovering at the margins of the decaying body politic.

We witness the staging of the classic existential predicament. If god or sovereign authority is absent, what indeed will transpire as the human will begins to control the affairs of daily life? An obsession to take charge of both negative and positive forces in his narrative, of both what's required and what's accidental, the necessary and the contingent, preoccupies the author. We see this combination of the utopian and the infernal first in the panorama of chaos envisioned by Simoun as he gazed at Intramuros from his surveillance outpost across the Pasig, the river symbolizing motion versus the immobility of the petrified urban surrounding:

"Within a few days," he murmured, "when from her four sides flames burn that wicked city, den of presumptuous nothingness and the impious exploitation of the ignorant and the unfortunate; when tumult breaks out in the suburbs and there rush into the terrorized streets my avenging hordes, engendered by rapacity and wrongdoing, then I will shatter the walls of your prison; I will snatch you from the clutches of fanaticism; white dove, you will be the phoenix that will be reborn from the glowing ashes....! A revolution plotted by men in obscurity tore me from your side. Another revolution will bring me to your arms, will revive me and that moon, before reaching the apogee of its splendor, will light the Philippines, cleaned of her repugnant refuse!" (*Fili* 207).

This hope of retribution (the body cure) through the amalgamation of terror, punishment of evil, restoration of justice, purification of the polluted body, and catharsis, is rendered poignantly in the images of the burning of Sodom, destruction of prisons, and the rebirth of the phoenix-like corpus of the community. In a world bereft of gods or any transcendent cosmic power, healing ensues after purgation of the toxic element and the salvation of the body through the collective sacrifice of humans making their own history. Such is the passage of the avenging angels of "the wretched of the earth" (to use Fanon's epithet for the colonized masses during the Cold War), the peasants and proletariat of "the third world," the majority of the planet's residents.

Paradigm Metamorphosis

At this juncture, I propose a decentering of Rizal's two novels by shifting our attention from Padre Florentino's sermon to Rizal's prayer and apostrophe to his country at the end of Chapter 23, "A Corpse." Chased and shot by the *guardia civil,* Ibarra's body disappears in the lake; but here, the *corpus delicti* surfaces to disturb the peace. Several chapters later, just before the planned "apocalypse" at the wedding feast takes place, news of Maria Clara's death is conveyed to Simoun by Basilio, the youthful student who represents the victims of the guilt-stricken system and the hope of the salvation of the motherland. Reminiscent of the vision of a liberated, prosperous homeland at the end of "The Philippines a Century Hence," Rizal takes hold of the floating signifier of Ibarra/Simoun, the duplicitous mediator of past and present, to interrupt the flow of the narrative. Here Rizal, through the critical musings of young Basilio, expresses with disarming intensity the task of the organic intellectual of the colonized, the mission of the critical intelligence: to remember the ordeals and sacrifices of the past generations in order to heal the break between nature and culture, the wound disjoining psyche and history. This moving farewell to Rizal's youthful past, to Leonor Rivera, all the victims of Calamba and other places. incorporating the fantasized advent of a paradisal future, calls for meditation with reference to the ultimate agenda of socialist revolution in the decades to come:

And forgetting his studies, with his look wandering in space, he thought of the fate of those two beings: he, young, rich, lettered, free, master of his destiny, with a brilliant future ahead of him, and she, beautiful like a dream, pure, full of faith and innocence, cradled among loves and smiles, destined for a happy life, to be adored in the family and respected in the world, and yet, nevertheless, those two beings, full of love, of dreams and hopes; by a fatal destiny, he wandered around the world, dragged without respite by a whirlpool of blood and tears, sowing bad instead of doing good, dismantling virtue and fomenting vice, while she was dying in the mysterious shadows of the cloister where she had sought peace and may perhaps have encountered sufferings, where she had entered pure and without stain and expired like a crushed flower!

Sleep in peace, unhappy child of my unfortunate motherland! Bury in your grave the enchantments of your childhood, withered in their vitality! When a people cannot offer its virgins a peaceful home, the shelter of sacred liberty; when a man can only bequeath dubious words to his widow, tears to his mother and slavery to his children, you do well to condemn yourselves to perpetual chastity, choking within your breasts the seed of a cursed future generation!

Ah, you have done well, not to have to tremble in your grave hearing the cries of those who agonize in the shadows, of those who feel themselves with wings and yet are fettered, of those who choke themselves for lack of liberty! Go, go with the dreams of the poet to the region of the infinite, vestige of woman glimpsed in a beam of moonlight, whispered by the supple stalks of the canebreaks…. Happy she who dies wept for, she who leaves in the heart of those who love her, a pure vision, a sacred memory, not stained by common passions which ferment with the years!

Go, we will remember you! In the pristine air of our motherland, under her blue sky, over the waves of the lake which imprison mountains of sapphire and shores of emerald, in her crystalline streams which the bamboo-canes overshadow, the flowers border, and dragonflies and butterflies enliven with their uncertain and capricious flight as if playing with the wind, in the silence of our forests, in the singing of our creeks, in the diamond cascades of our waterfalls, in the resplendent light of our moon, in the sighs of our evening breeze, and all that in the end evoke the image of the beloved, we will see you eternally as we have dreamed about you: lovely, beautiful, smiling like hope, pure like the light and, nevertheless, sad and melancholy contemplating our miseries! (*Fili* 261-63).

Incarnated in the lost object of the beloved, the vision of a redeemed future blends with the image of antediluvian nature, the landscape of Rizal's youth in Laguna, the scene of his sensuous joy absorbing the fetishized jewelry (history and alienated labor congealed in commodities) peddled by Simoun, the spontaneous impulses of a childhood seeking to resuscitate the corpse of Maria Clara, embodiment of virtue, purity and *jouissance*. Allegorical realism, critique, and dialectical reason coalesce here in Rizal's aesthetic-political project of bringing out the submerged possibilities immanent in the self-contradictory reality of his society, of showing what the force-field of conflict harbors by way of transformative resources and hitherto undiscovered species reserves.

At the heart of this critique of colonial reality, Rizal wrestled with the question of justice, punishment, retribution. The moral predicament of how to restore order and harmony in his life by way of superseding *ressentiment*, revenge and remorse, obsessed him. There is no question about the goal, but the means and method are uncertain, contingent on unpredictable circumstances. How can the natural virtues of pre-Spanish society (inferred from his gloss on Morga) be restored? How can the suffering of innocent children, women, and other victims of theocratic greed and irrational authority be prevented? In the context of the novels and Rizal's life, how can the honor of Ibarra's family (condensed in the humiliation and torture of his father), the eviction of his family and other Calambans from their homes, and the ravishing of all that the clan holds sacred (Maria Clara, Juli, Sisa, women in general), be redeemed? After critique, judgment awaits the guilty in the name of all the innocent victims.

We face the central problem of our time. Can we still invoke "divine violence" or the intervention of providence and its surrogates in history in the form of explosions of popular resentment, as in the recent terrorism of extremists and the equally violent reaction of NATO and the U.S. quasi-fascist state? The recent phenomenon of flag-waving crowds cheering the execution of Osama Bin Laden by US military troops violating Pakistan's sovereignty stands as an exemplum. Observers have noted how the trauma of Sepember 11, 2001, demands this sequence of happenings. We return to an archaic regime of original sin, inquisition, exorcism, penitence, self-flagellation, catharsis.

Slavoj Zizek tries to rehabilitate the notion of resentment by quoting W.G. Sebald: "Resentment...[according to Jean Amery] 'nails everyone of us unto the cross of his ruined past.' Absurdly, it demands that the irreversible be turned around, that the event [Nazi Holocaust] be undone.' The issue then is not to resolve but to reveal the conflict" (2008, 189). Precisely what Rizal did by exposing the social cancer corrupting everyone, the evils of Spanish colonialism. Thus he affirms the right to resentment in a programmatic strategy of sensitizing the conscience of the multitude (*ilustrados* as well as plebeians, workers, peasants) and its future-oriented will to remember and settle accounts with their oppressors.

Following a counterhegemonic intuition, Zizek stresses the need to carry out the logic of justice by not usurping the role of God to forgive and forget. Revenge has a function in the political economy of humans exercising their freedom to reorganize a world gone awry and arrange things in a more humane and caring ecumene. He calls for revaluing a form of heroic resentment that refuses to compromise and accede to the conciliatory blandishments of any official "Truth Commission." Zizek elaborates:

When a subject is hurt in such a devastating way that the very idea of revenge according to *jus talionis* is no less ridiculous than the promise of the reconciliation with the perpetrator after the perpetrator's atonement, the only thing that remains is to persist in the "unremitting denunciation of injustice." …Resentment has nothing to do with the slave morality [Nietzsche condemned]….It stands rather for a refusal to 'normalize' the crime, to make it part of the ordinary/explicable/accountable flow of things, to integrate it into a consistent and meaningful life-narrative; after all possible explanations, it returns with its question: "Yes, I got all this, but nevertheless, *how could you have done it*? Your story about it doesn't make sense!" (2008, 189-90).

Paradoxically, the enigmatic figure of Simoun doesn't make sense—in general, he is mysterious, sinister, the *filibuster* with a thousand disguises (like the Edmond Dantes in Dumas' novel) who disrupts routine by mere circulation, surprising us with the multiple, alternating masks of disingenuous personae. But for Basilio and others, Simoun as the metamorphosed/transvalued Ibarra makes uncanny sense. His cunning subterfuge, his calculus of revenge, is foiled not by its betrayal and accidental discovery (like the Katipunan), but by the report of the death of Maria Clara, the symbol of the purity, honor, and communal joy of the past. That vanished ideal can no longer be recovered, as Rizal intimates when he eliminates the selfless protagonist Elias in the *Noli*, frustrates both Ibarra's and the students' liberal schemes, depicts the tragic killing of Tandang Selo by his grandson Carolino (Cabesang Tales' son), and finally leads Simoun to submit to Padre Florentino's ministry before committing suicide.

Such astute contrivance of narrative twists and the manipulation of coincidences may not all be happenstance. After all, they triggered the rise of the

Katipunan and the 1896 insurrection, discharging the animus of vengeance into an organized collective effort, even though punctuated and threaded through with spontaneous anarchic outbursts replete with other adventurist, putschist gestures. That whole landscape of the interregnum crisis reflects the vacillations and opportunism of the ilustrado and other elements of the middle stratum caught in multilayered antagonisms. Rizal's plot of settling accounts succeeds as critique, prying open the bowels of self-contradictory reality, and unleashing those dammed-up forces that will renew life and the inexhaustible potentiality of the human species at the turn of the century.

In Quest of Maria Makiling

We cannot pursue here the theme of emancipatory violence and its legitimation (as Zizek does in his treatise) within the complex problematic of means and ends, ethics and teleology, immanence and transcendence. The universal issues of justice, revenge, retribution and social harmony require a protracted investigation due to historical contingencies and human errors. Suffice it to conclude by moving the discourse to the terrain of the unsaid or unspeakable in contemporary exchanges, "the woman question."

Earlier we noted that Anderson, either ignorant or wrongheaded, stated that Rizal's main source of motivation and background for his novels derived from European incidents and intellectual debates. This is entirely false, as Richardson has shown with respect to the militant nationalism of the *movimiento insurreccional* led by Adriano Novicio in Pangasinan and Nueva Ecija in 1884 twelve years before Bonifacio's uprising. Between the Cavite mutiny and the Katipunan insurrection, at least one important sequence of incidents should be given priority.

On December 12, 1988, twenty young women of Malolos petitioned Governor General Weyler—the notorious terror of Calamba, later Cuba's "butcher"—for permission to establish a "night school" so that they might study Spanish under Teodoro Sandiko whose socialist background has been mentioned earlier. When a Spanish priest objected, Weyler junked the petition. But the women defied the friar's prohibition and mounted a courageous agitation, something completely new in the Philippine scene. Eventually they obtained government approval on condition that instead of Sandiko, their teacher would be Señorita Guadalupe Reyes. This incident stirred up local passions that reverberated up to Spain. Writing from Barcelona on Feb. 17, 1889, Marcelo del Pilar, the editor of *La Solidaridad*, asked Rizal to send a letter supporting the fearless women of Malolos. Although busy with annotating Morga's book in the British Museum in London, Rizal agreed and composed his famous letter in Tagalog, sending it to Del Pilar on Feb. 22, 1889. Apart from the proleptic "el ultimo adios" poem, this letter sums up the itinerary of Rizal's intellectual adventure. This *filibustero* did not delay or filibuster, as it were, converting this occasion as another mode of "revenge." It can be construed as an act of demystifying *ressentiment* by a critique of hypocrisy, idolatry, and religious bigotry, in defense of critical reason and militant humanism which recalls Spinoza and Erasmus, even Bartolome de las Casas.

Written three years before Rizal's return home and the founding of the *Liga*, this letter may be considered a benchmark document of the Filipino revolutionary archive. It distills the entire labor of his studies since his arrival in Spain in 1882, occurring two years after the printing of the *Noli* and two years before the completion of the *Fili*. In this act of communication, Rizal plays the spiritual mentor, fraternal counselor, and tribal sage all at once. It recapitulates ideas expressed in the Morga annotations, in the *Noli* and "The Indolence of the Filipinos," and presages the clash between the standpoints of Simoun and Basilio/Padre Florentino and their surrogates.

Central to the letter is the call to bravely assert collective autonomy and rational judgment, and use rational judgment and good will. Rizal advises them to follow what is reasonable and just, and carry out the prime duties of teaching honor to their children, loving one's fellow citizens and the native land. In that way, rid of ignorance and abject fear, one asserts one's dignity, courage, responsibility and honor. Tyranny and servitude are thereby prevented by the prudent cultivation of "the light of reason which God has mercifully endowed us." Sandwiched between the precepts specifically addressed to the maternal role of women and the maxim of neighborly love is Rizal's biting comments on avaricious friars and malicious Spaniards who mock native women who have shown hospitality and deference. It is this traduced and vilified honor of Filipina women that Rizal cannot let go, not because he aspires to be the model defender of women, a proto-feminist vanguard-party spokesman, but because he identifies the honor of Filipinas with the substance of the nascent *patria*, including that of the Malay race (Zaide 1984, 157). It is an identification enabled by the sensibility of the romantic idealist shaped by folk Catholicism, the archaic *babaylan* tradition, the deism of Voltaire and Rousseau, and the democratic-populist trends drawn from the Protestant Reformation and the Jacobin revolution in France.

What precipitated Rizal's exaltation of Spartan women as his paragon for his compatriots? In his letters and in the *Memorias,* we saw overwhelming proof of Rizal's passionate attachment to his mother. Such unusually intense mother-love engenders the negative: his recognition that women are victimized by the patriarchal order, in particular by the mercenary, hypocritical frailocracy. He himself was aware of his chauvinism, his occupying a problematic position, as shown in his over-scrupulous conduct toward a series of paramours up to Josephine Bracken (for the latter as Rizal's *alter ego*, see the intriguing essay of Dolores Feria [1968]). In several letters to his brother Paciano in 1883, Rizal displayed a more than superficial knowledge of prostitution and women's subordination in Spain and other European countries: "Women abound even more (here in Madrid) and it is, indeed, shocking that in many places they intercept men and they are not the ugly ones either" (1993, 89). Experience served as the great teacher of metropolitan truth for the erstwhile benighted colonial subject.

Ambeth Ocampo may have been unjustly criticized for his demythologizing brief that Rizal was acquainted with brothels. He cites Rizal's observation: "With respect to morality there are some who are models of virtue and innocence, and others who have nothing womanly about them except their dress or at most their sex. Rightly it has been said that the women in the South of Europe have fire in their veins. However, here prostitution is a little more concealed than at Barcelona, though no less unrestrained" (Rizal 1993, 89-90). When he traveled with his friend Dr. Maximo Viola, Rizal displayed eagerness to learn about the condition of these "*casas de palomas de bajo vuelo*" so as to combat the vice, "unnatural and anti-psychological" (to use the terms attributed to Rizal). Dr. Viola added that Rizal hinted to him that "he had never been in favor of obeying blindly the whims of nature when their call was not duly justified by a natural and spontaneous impulse." When the two friends arrived in Vienna in the course of their six-month travels, two years before the Malolos epistle, Dr. Viola confessed the hero's "slip": Rizal "encountered the figure of a temptress in the form of a Viennese woman, of the family of the Camellias or hetaeras of extraordinary beauty and irresistible attraction" (Ocampo 1990).

Rizal's concern is not so much with female virtue as with the maternal function/role and its incalculable effects. His stress on individual reason and autonomous will, equality and respect for each other, was needed to remove women from the influence of the religious orders; he invokes God's gift of natural reason to ward off the despotic authority of the friars and correct servile habits. Rizal then concentrates on the function of the mother as progenitor and educator/nurturer: "What offspring will be that of a woman whose kindness of character is expressed by mumbled prayers... It is the mothers who are responsible for the present servitude of our compatriots, owing to the unlimited trustfulness of their loving hearts, to their ardent desire to elevate their sons."

Deploying throughout organic metaphors of growth and fruition, Rizal emphasizes the mother's crucial role in shaping the infant: "The mother who can only teach her child how to kneel and kiss hands must not expect sons with blood other than that of vile slaves." Because mothers are "the first to influence the consciousness of man," Rizal exhorts them to "awaken and prepare the will of our children towards all that is honorable, judged by proper standards, to all that is sincere and firm of purpose, clear judgment, clear procedure; honesty in act and deed, love for the fellowmen and respect for God." That is a *desideratum* because the whole community cannot expect honor and prosperity "so long as the woman who guides the child in his steps is slavish and ignorant." Despite their strength and good judgment, however, the Filipina mother has become a slave, hoodwinked and tied, rendered pussilanimous. In a sudden leap, Rizal ventures a generalization: "The cause of the backwardness of Asia lies in the fact that there the woman are ignorant, are slaves; while Europe and America are powerful because there the women are free and well-educated and endowed with lucid intellect and a strong will." This explains his subsequent invocation of Spartan women as the models to imitate, notwithstanding his knowledge that their position is underwritten by an iniquitous slave system prevailing in classical antiquity.

The Mother of All Insurgencies

A suspicion disturbs the epistolary self-assurance. Rizal feels that the Malolos women will not listen to him because of his youth, so he submits seven instructions for their evaluation, repeating what he has already stated about the need for dignity, knowledge, independence and altruism. His fifth and sixth advice, however, sounds an alarming note of a fear of betrayal, together with hostility to the superstitious machinations of a "grossly mercenary" priesthood. The fifth proposition seems a warning: "If the Filipina will not change her mode of being, let her rear no more children, let her merely give birth to them. She must cease to be the mistress of the home, otherwise she will unconsciously betray husband, child, native land, and all." Apprehensively, however, Rizal withdraws his animus and insists on everyone's equality in enjoying the divine gifts of intelligence and rational judgment.

Rizal's final words may be interpreted as a cautionary reminder for those cast out of the aboriginal garden: "May your desire to educate yourself be crowned with success; may you in the garden of learning gather not bitter, but choice fruit, looking well before you eat because on the surface of the globe all is deceit, and the enemy sows seeds in your seedling plot" (1984, 332). Didactic teleology here blends moral realism with satire, impugning the "fathers" and appealing to a future regime of stalwart mothers as the supreme tribunal of national vindication.

We pose here an impertinent question: If the mothers—Sisa, Maria Clara's mother, and potential mothers like Juli, Salome, Paulita Gomez—fulfilled their role and the patriarchal order is reconfigured or entirely vanquished, would Ibarra/Simoun be conceivable in such a world? If not, then we return to the mirrored reality where the patriarchs exploited and oppressed everyone, making rational motherhood difficult if not dangerous and thus proscribed. But can justice, revenge as payment for debts incurred, an eye for an eye as the fit compensation, be achieved by reviving mother-right (as Bachofen and Briffault once speculated [Hays 1958])?

Let us turn to a classical template that Rizal surely studied. In Aeschylus' trilogy, *The Oresteia*, the Erinyes or Furies that pursued Orestes for slaying his mother Clytemnestra represent the rule of tribal society; his matricide is settled by the Areopagus, the newly established court in the patriarchal city of Athens where Athena (sprung fully armed from Zeus's head), frees Orestes of his guilt and terminates the curse. The mandate of heaven is realized. The avenging Furies are propitiated by being made the city's protectors. Meanwhile, Zeus' appointment of Athena and Apollo may be construed as the supremacy of justice (moral retribution) and compassion. But instead of reinstating mother-right or equality of men and women, what supervenes is the rule of the landed aristocracy which, as the historian George

Thomson points out, occupies an intermediate position between the primitive tribe and the democratic city-state. The court was still dominated by the old patriarchal nobility exercising the duty of purification assigned by the Delphic oracle. However, the oath administered in the Areopagus invokes the Semnai, a trinity of female divinities, the presiding deities descended from the Erinyes (Thomson 1968, 272). These female spirits are subsumed in the figure of Spartan mothers whom Rizal summons and propitiates, not mother Spain, as muses of the project of national redemption (in 1896, Spanish women cheered Rizal's death; see Craig 1913, 145).

This somewhat neglected masterpiece of communicative action in the Rizal archive, if read contextually, can sharpen our appreciation of Rizal's materialist dialectics in practice. It demonstrates Rizal's sensitively calibrated merging of flexible tactics and principled strategy in liberating the colony from feudal barbarism and the trauma of religious servitude. It compels us to reorient our thinking so as to give priority to the agenda of gender equality, of combating sexism and female subordination, as the keystone of any emancipatory program of the progressive bloc. It combines Rizal's intransigent critical sensibility with the emancipatory drive that, in its allegorical dynamism, informs (among other projects) his recreation of the folkloric spirit of the nature goddess Maria Makiling (*La Solidaridad,* Dec. 31, 1890).

The goddess Maria Makiling personifies the once fabled harmony of humans and their natural habitat in a utopian golden age, the cooperative alliance of a still unspoiled nature and the tribal grassroot practices sketched by Rizal in his unfinished novel "The Ancient Tagalog Nobility." Spurned by a human lover escaping military conscription, this bountiful virgin of the mountain and forest disappears from sight; the alienation dividing nature and the world of the fathers afflicts everyone, rendering normal life arid, hollow, hopeless. Maria's Eden is lost, become mythical or utopian for the "unhappy consciousness" of modernity (for a contemporary report on the Rizal-Makiling connection, see Lahiri 1999). She bids farewell to her human lover: "Inasmuch as you have had no courage either to face a hard lot to defend your liberty and make yourself independent in the bosom of these mountains; inasmuch as you have had no trust in me, ...I deliver you to your fate, live and struggle alone; live as you can" (1962, 109). This curse/fate of abandonment by a mother-deity, evoking the image of Rizal's mother thrown in jail or his family driven out of their Calamba homes, is the object of Rizal's revenge, the pretext for Simoun's chiliastic fervor and eschatological musings.

Ultimately the dream of return to the legendary past of the mothers and the retribution for the crimes of the fathers may illuminate Apolinario Mabini's insight into the felicitous wedding of necessity and freedom, history and will, in our hero's incommensurable odyssey of exile and homecoming. Uncannily, death and eros converge in this suturing of *patria* and memory-fleshed place, as it did throughout the lover's elegiac call for embraces and kisses from Filipinas in his last farewell. Here is Mabini's tribute to Rizal: "In truth the merit of Rizal's sacrifice consists precisely in that it was voluntary and conscious. From the day Rizal understood the misfortunes of his native land and decided to work to redress them, his vivid imagination never ceased to picture to him at every moment of his life the terrors of the death that awaited him" (quoted in Quibuyen 1999, 62-63). From his vantage point of exile in Guam because of refusing allegiance to the American colonizers, Mabini urged his countrymen to imitate Rizal's virtues, just as Rizal, in his temporary refuge in Madrid, encouraged the women of Malolos to acquire those virtues of courage, rationality, compassion and perseverance without which a life of human dignity and freedom is not possible on earth.

SISA'S VENGEANCE:
RIZAL & THE "WOMAN QUESTION"

Liberty is a woman who grants her favors only to the brave. Enslaved peoples have to suffer much to win her, and those who abuse her lose her....Les femmes de mon pays me plaisent beaucoup, je ne m'en sois la cause, mais je trouve chez-elles un je ne sois quoi qui me charme et me fait rever [The women of my country please me very much. I do not know why, but I find in them I know not what charms me and makes me dream.]

--Jose Rizal, Epistolario Rizalino; Diary, Madrid, 31 March 1884

Religious misery is at once the expression of real misery and a protest against that real misery. Religion is the sign of the hard-pressed creature, the heart of a heartless world, the spirit of unspiritual conditions. It is the opium of the people.... After the earthly family is discovered to be the secret of the holy family, the former must then itself be criticized in theory and revolutionized in practice.

–Karl Marx," Introduction to the Critique of Hegel's Philosophy of Right" (1843) and "Theses on Feuerbach" (1845)

More than his persona as the astute and circumspect dissident, Jose Rizal as lover, romantic protagonist, and simpatico confidant of women of various nationalities, has preoccupied many scholars to the point of suspecting that there was something anomalous somewhere. Was Rizal manic-depressive, or simply neurotic? Few would accuse him of being an unscrupulous and promiscuous Casanova, much less a cynical Don Juan. In fact, Rizal was courtly, thoughtful, even fearful and wary toward the opposite sex—except his mother. What did he think of his friend Juan Luna's killing of his wife and mother-in-law? We do not really know, we can only speculate. The inamorata Leonor Rivera exposed the Rizal phallus as a "semblance" (to use the Lacanian rubric) while Josephine Bracken restored it to its decorous size. Only one other woman challenged him: Nelly Boustead, while the Japanese Seiko Usui/O-Sei-San confirmed his virility, sacrificing herself (in his judgment) without demanding any reciprocity nor due recognition of her gift/service.

Entangled in this seductive chronicle of amorous affairs, we take a moment to interpose mindful distance and ask: what is Rizal's ultimate assessment of women's actual virtue and potential? None of his biographers has contributed anything substantial on this, perhaps intimidated that if they venture to engage with "the woman question," they would provoke a Pandora's box of adversarial criticism that might expose vulnerable biases and unconscionable presumptions.

We dare to cross the threshold of forbidden and dangerous territory at this historic conjuncture of manifold crises in our homeland. The principles of feminism and women's liberation have rooted themselves firmly in civil society since the Sixties, emblematized by organizations such as Gabriela and its party-list, among others. And so we can carry on a discourse on gender equality, patriarchy, and sexual difference without recapitulating foundationalist origins (Aguilar 1988; Chant and McIlwaine 1995). Arguments about women's position in the social division of labor have progressed to the point where Maria Mies (1986) posits women's role in the production and reproduction of life as relatively independent from the production of goods, wages, profit, thus requiring a materialist analysis of its own. Frigga Haug (1999) reminds us that the feminist standpoint is both unscathing critique of ideology and utopian celebration of sensuous bodily joy, universalist solidarity, and collective self-determination, after the abolition of genders and the humanization of nature. Meanwhile, ludic or supremacist feminists (Ebert 1996; Hogan 2000) have valorized the "feminine" as a subversive sign of "desire" interrogating patriarchy, foregrounding in the process women's desiring-production as the singular agent of transforming society and emancipating humanity.

Framing the Question

It would be disingenuous not to recognize outright Rizal's limits as symptomatic determinations imposed by the subaltern, creole society and culture of his time. But, alternatively, one may hypothesize that Rizal was perhaps the first Filipino nationalist to have appropriated, if not resurrected, the body and its constellation of desires as a vehicle for grasping our collective "being-in-situation," simultaneously object and subject of thought. The colonized native was both active and passive, interpellated by conflicting discourses and practices; hence the dialogic and heteroglossic discourse of Rizal's satires, essays, narratives (in particular, *Makamisa*), together with the play of memory, perceptions, and fantasies in his letters and memoirs. He wove in his discourse elements of the sentient flesh, speaking subjects sutured in the diverse field of modalities of overlapping life-forms. He succeeded in capturing the truly overdetermined social formation of the Philippines constituted by antagonistic, residual and emergent modes of production.

From the perspective of object-relations psychoanalysis, Rizal's Oedipal complex quickly evaporated after his first romance, opening up for intervention the maternal/libidinal realm of invention, accident, and experimentation. Before the Dapitan exile, he was willing to explore the possibility of recreating Calamba in Sandakan, the British-controlled territory of Borneo, formerly owned and governed by the Muslim Sultanate of Sulu. He was both realistic and adventurous, critical and hospitable to the strange, enigmatic, and alien. Phallogocentric and moribund frailocracy, however, foiled all his schemes.

Colonial-theocratic sovereignty fixated Filipino women (the template of Rizal's dreams) in the patriarchal household economy. It compelled Rizal to wrestle with the challenge of discovering ways of altering their subaltern marginalization and subordination. He tried to usher his sisters and other female compatriots into the political/public sphere (for example, schooling, shared conversations in civic gatherings, and other modes of communal praxis) to thwart the oppressive privatization of their bodies and psyches. The *Liga* was his aborted project. Thus, instead of placing the erotic/libidinal in quarantine, Rizal reinscribes their subversive impulses into the terrain of political discourse where they mix and explode in the people's unceasing struggle for hegemony (moral leadership, intellectual authority) and institutional power. Women's madness and excesses represented in Rizal's novels symbolize and herald this eventuality. Without the affiliation and participation of women in the Filipino liberation struggle, the nation-in-the-making would simply reproduce gender and class inequality as well as racialist/imperialist domination.

Partly freed from the stranglehold of Rousseau and Enlightenment dogmas, Rizal reworked instinctively the utopian-socialist tendencies found in Olympe de Gouges, Fourier, Wollstonecraft, Marx and Engels (Macey 2000). They forecast the emergence of such exemplary figures as Teresa Magbanua, Gregoria de Jesus, Melchora Aquino, Trinidad Tecson, Salud Algabre, and others. But before we move on to Alexandra Kollontai, Rosa Luxemburg, Simone de Beauvoir, Juliet Mitchell, Angela Davis and other theoreticians of feminist identity/difference, we need to situate Rizal in the concrete social formation of colonial Philippines and define the conceptual framework in which Rizal's attitude and ideas on women's position can be judged for its prescience and synergetic potential. Thus we go back to Marx and Engels and the historical-materialist orientation in which the politics of Eros can be intelligibly understood in its totality, singular potency, and practical efficacy.

In the now classic treatise, *The Origin of the Family, Private Property and the State* (1844; 1891), Frederick Engels formulated the cardinal insight that the inequality of the sexes coincided with the rise of class society: "The overthrow of mother right was the world-historical defeat of the female sex" (1972, 120). Within the patriarchal monogamous family based on private property (land, domesticated animals, slaves), Engels added, "the woman was degraded and reduced to servitude; she became the slave of his lust and a mere instrument for the production of children." Women were relegated to the private sphere of the kitchen and boudoir under male authority. Historically, the form of patriarchal supremacy is a result of the class contradictions prevailing at a particular stage of social development, from savagery to slave, feudal and capitalist stages.

The anthropologist Robert Briffault noted that with the institutionalization of monogamous marriage and the nuclear family as the basic economic unit, the supremacy of the male became normative; the male head of household production with property-holding rights and the privilege of disposing surplus wealth displaced the mother. Structural coercion based on the male's inalienable right to property defined women's differential access to resources and their unequal life-chances. Integrally central in maintaining early tribal communal relationships, women lost their equal share in productive tasks and with it that acephalous solidarity gutted by "the rise of competitive interests," by commodity fetishism and the cash-nexus (Hays 1958, 179-80; Caudwell 1971). With the onset of capitalism, males became the bourgeois masters, women the proletarian class within the family.

Revisiting the Matrix

In pre-Hispanic Philippines, residual mother-right flourished within extended kinship groups (gens or clans) engaged in hunting, fishing, and subsistence farming in communally managed territory. Production was chiefly for use, not for exchange. In those self-provisioning communities, there was no substantial surplus; women inherited property and exercised a large degree of autonomy. Women's productive function in gathering food, fishing, planting/harvesting. domestic and artisanal crafts (weaving, pottery, etc.) gave them economic independence and parity with men. In reviewing the status of native women before and after the conquest, Elizabeth Eviota observes that women producers controlled their own labor and its fruits, while "unmarried women exercised their sexuality freely...Women were the valued people exchanged in the marriage transaction" supervised by kins and the whole community (1992, 35-36). Women's active role in production and reproduction allowed them to be relatively sovereign thinking, enjoying subjects endowed like men with the human-species potential actualizable through cooperative sensuous praxis.

Spanish colonialism destroyed that egalitarian communal setup. It ushered a thoroughgoing gender differentiation with the institutionalization of private property, monogamy, and the patriarchal authority of fathers within the family. The cloistering of women within the male-dominated household limited them mainly to accomplishing religious and household duties. Onerous tribute of unpaid labor reduced the natives to debt peonage, the root of the iniquituous patron-client tie-up that legitimizes inequality across race, class, and gender. With the church regulating women's bodies/sexuality and imposing a regime of chastity, women displaced from work and driven to prostitution or vagrancy were confined to convents and public jails, or deported to Palawan.

Rizal depicted the methodical surveillance of women (chiefly via the confession as the disciplinary, therapeutic technique) in the plight of Dona Victorina, Dona Consolacion, Maria Clara, Sisa, Juli, Paulita Gomez, among others. Eviota concludes: "Centuries of economic, political and religious imposition had transformed the lively sexual assertiveness of Filipino women into a more prudish, cautious image of womanhood" (1992, 61). The church-sanctioned institutions of monogamous marriage and the colonial State's routinization of charisma (Gurvitch 1971) sealed the final demise of "mother-right," with the *babaylan*s reduced to witches or malignant *brujas*. The fate of Maria Clara encapsulates the loss of status of women of the emerging *principalia*, and of the more intense pacification of her lesser sisters in the symbolic-ideological template of a racialized patriarchal society. Nonetheless, those who refused marriage or violated/resisted the despotic family—Ibarra, Elias, Salome, Basilio, Tasio, Cabesang Tales, and others—presaged a salvific and reconciling utopian future for all since the social contract depended on unchallenged male ascendancy.

Within this historical-materialist framework, we can properly appreciate Rizal's works as articulations of a synthesizing theoretical inquiry in which the form of universality springs from the concrete singularity of particular life-worlds (Oizerman 1981). Social totality acquires concrete dynamics in the lived experience of sensuous reflective subjects. Aesthetically, they render typical what are specific and individual. The predicament of Maria Clara, Sisa, Salome, Juli, Dona Consolacion and other characters in Rizal's novels becomes emblematic of the decaying colonial order of nineteenth-century Philippines. In depicting the physiognomies and symptomatic acts of his female protagonists, Rizal also presented a lucid anatomy of the body politic, the diseased corpus for which he was imploring his audience to suggest a cure. In short, the key to understanding Rizal's revolutionary critique of colonial society may be found in his realistic-allegorical delineation of women in his fiction and discourse. By symbolic extrapolation, Rizal shows how patriarchal supremacy founded on the control of women's bodies and their productivity becomes the ultimate "weak link" in the colonial class/race hierarchy the toxic vestiges of which still afflict us today (epitomized among others by the Catholic Bishops' opposition to the Comprehensive Reproductive Rights Bill [HB 4244] being proposed in the Philippine Congress).

Orthodox/Heterodox Enunciations

In a much anthologized essay "The Filipino Woman" (1952) written at the height of the Cold War, Carmen Guerrero Nakpil elaborated a notion of the Filipino woman as a heterogeneous, multifaceted, amphibious creature that seems to inhabit not those tropical islands in Southeast Asia but some kaleidoscopic realm of fantasy. Not that she defied history or geography; in fact, she dared to encompass both by presenting a hybrid, polychromatic portrait. It is a sophisticated attempt to capture the variegated position of Filipino women in history, offering us a pretext to explore Rizal's thinking about women, sexuality, gender, and everyday life in the context of anticolonial resistance. If prisons, for Dostoevsky, index the truthful condition of any society, then the situation of women may be considered the revealing symptom of the health or malaise of their habitat, both its sociohistorical and psychic configuration.

Nakpil is a liberal but dilettantish observer of Filipino manners and mentalities. She is careful to discriminate fact from fiction: "Although, historically, it would be inaccurate to go so far as to maintain, as many writers like Rizal and Craig have, that amazonian princesses like Urduja and autocratic matriarchs like Sima once ruled over Filipinos..., [what] these pretty tales of displaced queens seek to symbolize was nonetheless solid and substantial reality." The truth, however, involved a more elaborate, complex interweaving of hierarchical gender-differentiated and autonomous spheres (Eviota 1992). After the Spaniards converted the indigenous barangays and made the Filipina "preoccupied with fig leaves," Rizal and his nineteenth century contemporaries had to go to Europe "to get a good look at women."

Rizal's women were classified legally by the Spanish regime together with infants and idiots, Nakpil adds, "for she could neither enter into contracts without her husband's consent, if married, nor leave her home without her parents' consent before 25, if unmarried." That applies of course to upper-class women. She concludes that the Filipino woman of the period just after World War II is "a sort of compromise between the affected little Christian idealist of the Spanish regime, the self-confident go-getter of the American era, and the pagan naturalist of her Asiatic ancestors" (1980, 14). From this mixture of lifestyles and essentialized ingredients, Nakpil supposes that in a few generations, the Filipino woman will iron out her "mongrel contradictions" into a 'thoroughbred homogeneity" embodied in a "clear, pure, internally calm, symmetrical personality." But she resists such a possibility. Why? Because then she "will have lost the infinite unexpectedness, the abrupt contrariness, the plural unpredictability which now make her both so womanly and so Filipino" (1980,18). Ludic postmodernism takes over empirical realism.

We thus confront a creature both womanly and Filipino despite circumstances and contingencies. But is this gendered construct real or imagined? In the midst of the rancorous debate over the Reproductive Health Bill, we wonder whether Nakpil's image of the polymorphously perverse, composite Filipina body is causing all the furor and controversy. Is this aleatory, contrarious, unpredictable group the pretext, topic, occasion or effect of what is happening? As the comparatist anthropologist Jack Goody has demonstrated, the historical status of women in any society depends on the nuanced articulation of the family, cultural specifics, and the politico-economic system, in which a degree of structural autonomy may exist between production and reproduction: patriarchal authority in politics, matrilineal power in the domestic domain, and various permutations of kinship and sexual division of labor (1998, 95).

An analogous controversy bedevils the position of women in Rizal's discourse that makes problematic their catalyzing or counter-bewitching resonance in his life (more on witches later). This is not virginal territory to explore. All the Rizal biographies cannot avoid mentioning, if not belaboring, the propaedeutic influence of his mother Teodora Alonso, Leonor Rivera, and Josephine Bracken, not to forget the shadowy Segunda Katigbak and the vibrant Nelly Boustead hovering over the margins of his memoirs. But from this distance in time and space, it is self-indulgent to speculate on the erotic, libidinal adventures of the hero—unless we intend to package that aura of romantic melodrama for sale to the profit-maximizing mass media. Are we not reeling from a surfeit of these banalities and trivia?

For our purpose of doing an experiment in thought/critique about the function of the female/feminine in Rizal's thought and its reverberations in ideological struggle, this essay will be limited to a focus on one question: Was Rizal (his life and works) a contributor to the maintenance of the patriarchal order or a critic of the effects of the social division of labor in class society, which is the condition of possibility for male supremacy, sexist chauvinism, and the exploitation and oppression of women? Are characters such as Sisa, Maria Clara, Salome and Juli significant for more than their technical efficacy in the melodramatic twists of the narrative? What ultimately is the role of Josephine Bracken in the sequence of women-protagonists in Rizal's life beginning with, say, Segunda Katigbak? What follows are speculative glosses and heuristic reflections, a cognitive mapping of the subject-position of this "Other" whose subliminal tracks were already outlined by Nakpil's versatile pen.

Syndrome of the Ideal

Most discussions of Rizal's women usually start with Maria Clara and her counterpart in real life, Leonor Rivera. Let us not tarry with the first whose value as a model was fully assayed first by Salvador P. Lopez in his "Maria Clara—Paragon or Caricature?" in *Literature and Society* (1940), and put to rest in the trenchant critical inventory of Dolores Feria's "The *Insurrecta* and the *Colegiala*" (1968). Of the informed Rizal commentators, only Nick Joaquin seems to be scandalous enough to salvage Maria Clara from the Victorian cesspool. Joaquin urges us to read again Chapter 7, "Idyll in an Azotea," and pay close attention to the eyes of Maria Clara and Juan Crisostomo Ibarra, for "the question that love poses in a bright or veiled glance cannot be answered by speech" (1988, 11). But the encounter between the two lovers is not just optical; it is noisy, as it were, counterpointed by a plethora of ventriloquizing voices, not a conversation but spliced whispers of two solitary persons communing with conscience and gnomic spectral presences.

What is curious is that face to face with his beloved, Ibarra invokes the organ of memory where Maria Clara's image blends with the landscape of his journeys in Europe mixed with local scenery. Remembrance resurrects the past: Your memory "has been my comfort in the solitude of my soul in foreign countries; your memory has negated the effect of the European lotus of forgetfulness, which effaces from the remembrance of our countrymen the hopes and the sorrows of the Motherland." For the traveling native, the beloved has metamorphosed into "the nymph, the spirit, the poetic incarnation of my country: lovely, simple, amiable, full of candor, daughter of the Philippines, of this beautiful country which unites with the great virtues of Mother Spain the lovely qualities of a young nation" (2004, 58). For the expatriate fabulist, the local muse Maria Makiling is just around the corner.

Idealization sanitizes the submerged furies of envy and jealousy. Amidst this elaborate rhetoric of denying that Ibarra has forgotten her sweetheart, the past returns in the farewell letter he wrote, which she reads to remind him of "pleasant quibbles, alibis of a bad debtor." The demure, acquiescent paramour revives the admonishing tone of Ibarra's father, with a message recalling the mother's death and the father's impending demise, and the need to sacrifice the present for a "useful tomorrow for you and your country." This patriarchal command, transmitted through the son's fiancee, agitates Ibarra and compels this retort: "You have made me forget that I have my duties" to honor the dead. Agreed, Maria Clara was not "a namby-pamby Manang," as Joaquin chides us; and that her confessor found her a problem girl. Nonetheless, she is only a mediating instrument for Ibarra to satisfy the traditional demands of filial piety and vindicate the honor of the ancestral totems. In the end, she is used by Padre Damaso (her biological father) to humiliate Ibarra by forcing the cuckold Capitan Tiago to marry her to another man, Linares.

Residual matrilineality soon asserts itself. When Ibarra returns after his escape from the *guardia civil* to see Maria Clara for the last time, he renews his vow by figuratively restoring the power of mother-right: "By my dead mother's coffin, I swore to make you happy no matter what happened to me. You could break your own pledge, she was not your mother, but I who am her son, I hold her memory sacred and despite a thousand perils, I have come here to fulfill my pledge..." (2004, 532). For her part, Maria Clara reveals the secret of her origin—the friar's violation of Capitan Tiago's trust and her mother Pia Alba, the break-up of the illusion of the Indio father's authority—and her promise not to forget her oath of fidelity. The inscrutable becomes legible by oral mediation. This scene follows Elias' renunciation of the patriarchal mandate to uphold the tarnished family honor by refusing to take revenge on Ibarra and allow the unity of all the victims seeking justice to supersede his clan's particularistic interest. Nonetheless, Maria Clara serves throughout as the seductive screen of the fathers and the dutiful sons.

Witness to Emergencies

By the time Rizal was born in 1861, the predominantly feudal/tributary mode of production was already moribund and an obstacle to further socioeconomic development. Trade and commerce expanded when the country was opened to foreign shipping in 1834-1865, especially after the completion of the Suez Canal in 1869 (Arcilla 1991). Vestiges of courtly love and chivalric ways dissolved in the triumph of the cash-nexus warranted by merchant and circulation capital, further validating profitable marital exchanges to expand or consolidate property. A national market arose. While the islands for the most part remained tribal and rural under the grip of the rent-collecting frailocracy and its subaltern *principalia*, land-tilling families such as those of Rizal flourished within the limits of the colonial order. The family household organization enabled the socially constructed gender asymmetry based on biological difference to segregate daughters from sons (women assigned to procreation and child nurturance, men to public affairs) and adversely affect their potential to develop as creative human beings and morally responsible citizens.

Political power continued to be monopolized by the peninsulars in the bureaucracy and military, together with the religious orders. They controlled large estates and appropriated the social wealth (surplus value or profit) produced by the majority population of workers and peasants most of whom were coerced under law (for example, the *polo servicios*) and reduced to slavish penury. Ruthless pauperization also doomed indigenous folk deprived of access to public lands, animals, craft tools, and so on. Only a tiny minority of creoles and children of mixed marriages (*mestizos* of Chinese descent) were allowed to prosper under precarious, serf-like, and often humiliating conditions that eventually drove them to covert or open rebellion. Rizal was one of these children sprung from the conjuncture of contradictory modes of production and reproduction of social relations, a child responding to the sharpening crisis of the moribund, decadent Spanish empire.

Rizal's family belonged to the *principalia*, the town aristocracy. His parents owned a large sumptuous stone house and adjacent property; their wealth derived from cultivating leased land owned by the Dominican Order which later expelled them for refusal to accede to a rental increase and other impositions. Rizal's mother managed a store and operated a flour-mill and ham press; the parents traced their lineage to merchants and provincial officials with affluent Chinese petty-bourgeois provenance (see Chapters 2-4 in Craig 1913). With a private library of more than 1,000 volumes (the largest in Calamba, Laguna), the Rizals (of eleven children, nine were women) enjoyed a relatively privileged rank among the native *gente*s or clan establishment. Compared to his muted respect for his father, Rizal esteemed his "clairvoyant" mother in a more expressive and exuberant way: "My mother is a woman of more than ordinary culture; she knows literature and speaks Spanish better than I. She corrected my poems and gave me good advice when I was studying rhetoric. She is a mathematician and has read many books" (1938, 335). Intellectually more adept than her husband and belonging to a more distinguished clan of professionals, Teodora Alonso (Rizal complained in the same letter to Blumentritt) "did not want that I should study more!"

Later on, in an 1884 letter copied by Leonor Rivera, Rizal's mother would advise him not to "meddle in things that will distress me," congratulating him on his graduation: ""I'm thanking our Lord for having bestowed on you an intelligence surpassing that of others" (1993, 159). But she wryly cautions him not to be too wise: "If he gets to know more, the Spaniards will cut off his head." Confident and proud of his accomplishments at the

Ateneo and in Europe, Rizal set the warning aside. No doubt Rizal worshipped his mother; consequently, when she was subjected by Calamba's *gobernadorcillo* and *guardia civiles* to the cruel punishment of walking from Calamba to Santa Cruz, a distance of 50 kilometers, on a charge that was never substantiated, Rizal suffered an incalculably profound trauma. It was a deeply painful wound that disturbed him enough to motivate him to condemn—to quote his rationale for writing his novels—"our culpable and shameful complacence with existing miseries," and "to wake from slumber the spirit of the Fatherland." The mother's ordeal served as the primal scenario of violation, the initiation into the crucible of Rizal's life-pilgrimage. It also marked the defeat of the Indio fathers—their virtual emasculation and castration—and the return of the avenging Furies of classical natural law.

Rizal was then only eleven years old when his mother was arrested on that malicious charge. She and her brother Jose Alberto, a rich Binan ilustrado, were accused of trying to poison the latter's wife who abandoned his home and children when the husband was on a business trip in Europe. It was Teodora Alonso who persuaded the brother to forgive his wife's infidelity, to no avail; she connived with the Spanish lieutenant of the Guardia Civil to file a case in court accusing her husband and Dona Teodora of trying to kill her. Rizal's recounting of the disaster (in the *Memorias* entry from Jan. 1871 to June 1872) does not wholly capture the devastating impact of this disaster on the adolescent's psyche: "The mayor....treated my mother with contumely, not to say brutality, afterward forcing her to admit what they wanted her to admit, promising that she would be set free and re-united with her children if she said what they wanted her to say....My mother was like all mothers: deceived and terrorized..." (1950, 30).

Rizal visited her in prison; she endured the unjust imprisonment for two years and half. With his brother also suspected of complicity with Father Jose Burgos, executed with Fr. Gomez and Fr. Zamora for sedition, Rizal summed up the effect of the two events: "From then on, while still a child, I lost confidence in friendship and mistrusted my fellowmen." Leon Maria Guerrero rightly appraised this unbearable tragedy of his mother as the key pivotal experience that Rizal could not face except through the anonymous student diary we quoted. He grappled with it through the cathexis of a public grievance, the 1872 martyrdom of the three secular priests which tormented his brother Paciano, "not so agonizing or so personal as his beloved mother's shame,...shamefully imprisoned, unfairly tried and unjustly condemned" (1969, 17; see Baron-Fernandez 1980, 19-20). Such injustice implied the loss of an objective standard of morality; the teleology of scholastic metaphysics gave way to the contingency, relativism and perspectivism of the modern world where force and material power settled disputes and adjudicated antagonisms.

Deciphering Eve's Stigmata

To resolve the trauma, Rizal invented female characters whose struggles sublimated his mother's experience and its painful affects. Sisa's plight may be read as Rizal's attempt to confront the violation of his mother's honor by indirection and to redress the grievance. But one apprehends an excess in the narrative, more obsessive than melodramatic, more exorbitant than the rhetorical pity and fear evoked by Aristotelian tragedy. In Chapter 21 of the *Noli*, the *guardia civiles* arrest Sisa as the "mother of thieves," blaming her for her children's actions. The mother is thus made answerable and responsible for her sons, not the delinquent father. Sisa's walk to the barracks is Rizal's re-enactment of his mother's torture, an unforgivable outrage. It was not just an empathetic re-living of the mother's agony but a mimetic performance of the ordeal. This actualization may be construed as a cathartic effort to assuage the compulsion to repeat the past:

Seeing herself marching between the two, she felt she could die of shame. It is true no one was in sight, but what about the breeze and the light of day? True modesty sees glances from all sides. She covered her face with her handkerchief and thus, going on blindly, she wept bitterly in humiliation. She was aware of her misery. She knew she had been abandoned by all including her own husband, but until now she had considered herself honorable and respected; until now she had regarded with compassion those women shockingly attired whom the town called the soldiers' concubines [Dona Consolacion, the alferez's wife, and Don Alberto's deviant and vindictive wife would represent this group]. Now it seemed to her that she had descended one level lower than these in the social scale (2004, 166).

Sisa's intense shame attests to the power of gendered socialization primarily mediated through the family and the church apparatus, as Rizal would argue in his letter to the Malolos women. But Sisa's sense of honor testifies to an inherent dignity, an impregnable self-respect—qualities he recommends for Filipina women to acquire—testifying to her goodness and decency despite sordid appearances. Sisa's torment accelerates when this dweller on the fringes beyond the scope of the church bells' tolling (measuring the extent of Spanish power) approaches the town: "she was seized with terror; she looked in anguish around her: vast rice fields, a small irrigation canal, thin trees—there was not a precipice or a boulder in sight against which she could smash herself." Sisa then becomes suicidal as the urban space engulfs her. Alienated from the urban circuit of money and commodity exchange, she is terrified by the signs of civilization. Inwardly she vows to her son that they will withdraw farther into "the depths of the forest." When she reminds the soldiers that they have entered the town, Rizal's discourse becomes opaque, generalized, imposing rhetorical distance: "Her tone could not be defined. It was a lament, reproach, complaint: it was a prayer, pain and grief, condensed into sounds" (167). Inside the barracks, "she was convulsed with bitter sobbing—a dry sobbing that was tearless and without words." Literary artifice becomes impotent here to transcribe maternal anguish, the dissonant music of the pre-Oedipal *chora* (Kristeva 1986).

Sisa now resembles an animal, sensuous practice suspended in defensive pathos. Before she was released by the alferez who was at loggerheads with the friars, "Sisa passed two hours in a state of semi-imbecility, huddled in a corner, head hidden between her hands, hair disheveled and in disarray." She was summarily thrown out from the barracks, "almost forced out because she was too stunned to move." She is a non-entity to the alferez, a sensuous psyche consigned to the domain of inert objects and beasts, a figure caught in the antinomy between the transcendent and the phenomenal dimensions of human existence (Heller 1999, 229).

Reincarnations

What happens subsequently is Sisa's transformation into the voice of Nature, the sentient environment of rural Philippines. Conversely, it is the humanization of the stigmatized territory customarily identified with the autochtonous ambience of savagery and barbarism, with bandits or *tulisanes*, with outlaws, pagans and vagrant lunatics. With Sisa, however, Rizal describes the process of dehumanization/naturalization, beginning with her calling for her sons upon arrival at her hut, searching her surroundings: "Her eyes wandered with a sinister expression. They would brighten up now and then with a strange light; then they would darken like the skies during a stormy night. One can almost say that the light of reason was ebbing close to extinction." She wandered "screaming or howling strange sounds. Her voice had a strange quality unlike the sound produced by human vocal chords." Rizal deprives her of human language and endows her with the more infinitely varied sounds of the elements. The next day, defying the narrator's wish that "some kindly angel wing would blot out from her features and memory the ravages of suffering" and that Mother Providence would intervene during her sleep, "Sisa wandered aimlessly, smiling, singing or talking, communing with all of nature's creation," except her fellow humans.

In Rizal's poignant dramatization of this *topos* of *pieta* (mother-child linkage), Sisa commands a reservoir of psychic energy not found in the other female protagonists. It is not found in Juli, Cabesang Tales' daughter, whose labor-power had to be alienated when her father joins the outlaws. As though re-living the traumatic ordeal of Rizal's mother, the narrative voice describes Juli's walk to the convent accompanied by Sister Bali. "She thought the whole world was looking at her and pointing a finger at her." Overwhelmed with terror, she resisted Sister Bali's urging, "pale, her features contorted. Her look seemed to say that she saw death before her" (335). Frightened by the prospect of her lover Basilio's exile, with wrath and despair, Juli closed her eyes so as not to see the abyss into which she was going to hurl herself"—the desperate assertion of her freedom, a stoic defiance of woman's enslavement.

One can infer a general tendency from this incident, a hypothetical line of argument. When the family's patriarch can no longer protect the household with the separation of the worker from the means of production/subsistence, the daughter becomes a prey for the lecherous power lurking behind the institutional enclaves and indoctrinated practices. Pushed to the extreme, Juli preserves her dignity, her chastity, in her lethal escape from that profanation emanating from the house of God's ministers. This anticipates Maria Clara's prison of Santa Clara in Intramuros at the close of the *Noli* from which the only escape is madness or enigmatic silence and disappearance enforced by the carceral discipline of an obscurantist institution. Women's experience of self is thus structured in the tension between the hegemonic ideological representations and the unfulfilled needs of the sensuous, suffering body, repressed but still animated with its genuine wants and desires.

The Pathos of Excommunicating Truth

In contrast to Juli, Sisa is caught in a severe contradiction: she cannot kill herself because her sons need her. The maternal instinct compels communication with other victims. In the latter part of the *Noli*, we encounter Sisa again on the eve of the San Diego town festival when Maria Clara and her relatives confront the leper, a blind man "singing of the romance of the fishes..." Art and reality collide. The blind singer allegedly contracted leprosy by taking care of his mother. Rizal dilates on this episode of the leper who, like Sisa, uttered "strange incomprehensible sounds." When Sisa approached the leper sunk to his knees thanking Maria Clara for the spontaneous gift of her locket, what Rizal calls "a rare spectacle" dramatized here incorporates that germ of a universal principle growing out of the historically specific life-world of women in that reactionary milieu. It is the negated principle of woman's decisive function in reproduction, nurturance, and production of subsistence without which a regime of gender equality is impossible (see Ebert (1996).

This particular scene speaks volumes on the themes of justice, equality, egalitarian and participatory democracy, ecumenical peace, and ecological survival whose manifold ramifications we cannot spell out and analyze here. Notice the multilayered implications of the mad mother exhorting the blind leper to pray for the living on the day of the dead, this gesture of reconciling incompatibles deliberately punctuated by the clamor of the normal spectators to separate the two victims:

As he felt her contact, the leper cried out and jumped up. But the mad woman held on to his arm to the great horror of the bystanders, and said to him: "Let us pray!...pray! Today is the day of the dead! Those lights are the life of men; let us pray for my sons!"

"Separate them, separate them! The mad woman will get contaminated!" the crowd was shouting, but no one dared to approach them.

"Do you see that light from the tower? That is my son Basilio who comes down by a rope! Do you see that one from the convent! That is my son Crispin, but I am not going to see them because the priest is sick and has many coins of gold and the coins got lost. Let us pray, let us pray for the soul of the priest! I brought him *amargoso* and *zarzalidas*; my garden was full of flowers, and I had sons. I had a garden, I was taking care of flowers and I had two sons!" (2004, 249-50).

Of the various thematic strands and motifs woven in this network, I will only underscore three: 1) the horticultural stage of social production alluded to recalls the stage of the matrilineal/matrilocal setup in primitive society, a time when the communal household enabled the reciprocal division of labor between the sexes—notice the absence of Sisa's husband, her sole supervision of the household, and her subsistence obtained from working the land (productive labor as one form of praxis); 2) the parasitic excess of a mercantile economy (centered on coinage extracted by friars, thus combining religious ideology and trade/commerce) monopolized by a theocratic state and a frailocracy whose mercenary use of religion demystifies their legitimacy in purveying the mystical and magical; and, finally, 3) the contamination/contagion of an alienated society, misrecognized but actually lived by the people who called for the separation of the physically diseased and the psychically abnormal, both appendages of a cancerous body politic.

We cannot help but register the behavior of the crowd as cynical, callous and hypocritical. The spectacle manifests a further irony inscribed in the fact that the living have mortgaged their destinies to the dead—indeed, one can say that the dead fathers, tradition, fetishized rituals, idolized metals and reifying commodities (symbolized in the *File* by the hypnotic power of Simon's merchandise) have taken over. Aside from taxes and governmental levies on ordinary citizens, the selling of indulgences, and other ceremonial fees and tributes collected by the church demonstrates systemic corruption. In the last chapter taking place on Christmas Eve, Basilio catches up with his deranged mother. Finally she recognizes him and is briefly restored to normalcy, only to die and be consumed in a funeral pyre together with the fugitive Elias. Phoenix-like, Sisa's motherhood is affirmed only to be dialectically cancelled and preserved or sublated into the predicament of other surrogates and avatars—Melchora Aquino, Salud Algabre, Felipa Culala, Maria Lorena Barros, Cherith Dayrit, Luisa Posa-Dominado, Kemberley Jul Luna, and other militants in today's national-democratic insurgency. We still labor under the sharpening crisis of the imperial fathers and their native acolytes, alarmed by the resurgent nationalism of fiery woman-warriors, mothers and daughters of a long durable and sustainable revolutionary tradition authentically of our own making (Aguilar 1998; San Juan 1999).

Exorcising the "Two-faced Goliath"

We need not linger over the semantic and philosophical complexities of other episodes where Sisa intrudes. Suffice it to mention here the scene in Chapter 40 where Dona Consolacion, the alferez's crazed wife tortures Sisa; or in other episodes where Sisa's seemingly gratuitous appearances at the margin of festivities disrupt the quotidian trappings and ceremonies of the respectable citizens. As an antithesis to the maternal archetype (instanced by the negative examples of Maria Clara's mother, Dona Victorina de Espadana, and others), Dona Consolacion may be interpreted as the wicked half of the ambiguous duality of the mythical pair Demeter/Persephone, the Laura/Flerida duality in Francisco Balagtas' *awit*, or Kali, the Indian goddess of fertility and destruction (Eliade 1958, 418-19). Alterity operates within the gender dichotomy, as in all socially constructed categories of subject-positions, of identities. Dona Consolacion is a modified specimen of the genre. Isolated and frustrated, forbidden from participating in the festival ("she saturated herself in her own bile") and ready to unleash repressed energies on anyone in sight. We confront again the archaic Furies hounding the perpetrators and apologists of rape and matricide.

Rizal amplifies her Medusa-like malignance in a way complementary to Sisa's unnnatural look: "Her eyes glittered like a serpent's, caught and about to be crushed underfoot
. They were cold, luminous, piercing, akin to something slimy, filthy and cruel" (346). Is this the sensitive, devout Rizal repulsed by the loathsome aspect of the sinful Eve, the mesmerizing siren and wily temptress of myth and fable? Her unrelenting brutality toward Sisa who was reduced into an animal emitting "howling sounds" can

perhaps be understood as a release of dammed-up resentment against her husband; but what enables her to do this is her sharing the alferez's status evident in her taunt: "Cursed be the mother who gave you birth!" With equal fury, Dona Consolacion attacks her husband, blaming him for not allowing her "to fulfill my duties toward God!" This episode is a hilarious vaudeville of marital conflict and its reverberating tensions, as evinced in the case of Uncle Alberto cited earlier. Rizal satirized local mores and manners with gusto, somewhat diverting us from the real target of the degradation of both sexes; but the power of Rizal's critique ultimately inhered in the grasp of the totality of social relations, which subsumed the economic structures that buttressed the racializing ideology and institutional practices of Spanish colonial might. What is true and real in the lived experiences of Rizal's characters (as well as his contemporaries) acquire meaning and significance only within the context of the historical totality, in the dynamic sequence of the past moving to the present and future, in nineteenth-century Philippines.

The patriarchal age might be coming to an end, as Rizal once intoned; but its repressive legacy endured up to his death, and after. Dona Consolacion and her benign counterparts, such as Paulita Gomez and Dona Victorina, may be Rizal's strategy of thwarting feminist protest. After all, not all women conform to the Maria Clara/Leonor Rivera model. Early experiences involving Consuelo Ortigas, Leonor Valenzuela, Segunda Katigbak, the anonymous older L. of an adjacent village, not to mention the unstinting solicitude of his mother and sisters throughout his life, all offered Rizal comfort and affirmation of his virility in one degree or another; none threatened him or provoked an unconventional response. So whence the need to invent a nasty violent female protagonist, displaying her irrational fury and then neutralizing her by parody and caricature so as to guarantee our safety from her claims to rational judgment? Why exhibit women's aggressive capacity, her destructive potential? Why the need to exorcise the derelict, malevolent wife of uncle Alberto—if not to purge the devastating trauma of her mother's torture and compensate for the male Indio's powerlessness?

Unrequited love cannot justify any suspicion of Rizal's chauvinism. With Segunda Katigbak, it was Rizal's internal schism that paralyzed the adolescent male ego: "But at the critical moments of my life I have always acted against my heart's desire, obeying contradictory purposes and powerful doubts" (1950, 52). A schism of objective and subjective determinants erupts, signaling the subject's forced initiation into secular modernity. That crisis occurred in December 1881, six years before his engagement with Leonor Rivera was annulled by her parents who could dispose of their daughter's body without consulting her. Even though he enjoyed Nelly Boustead's company, among others, and succumbed to the O-Sei-San's insidious charm—addressing her in his diary, Rizal wrote that "No woman, like you, has ever loved me. No woman, like you, has ever sacrificed for me," not even his mother or his fiancee (Zaide 1984, 132), Rizal confessed that he almost grew mad when he lost Leonor. It was the "first sledgehammer blow" of the railway construction that fell on him; the British engineer Kipping was a free man, Rizal was not (1999, 113).

What was the lesson? What insight was Rizal imparting when he thwarted self-pity by proclaiming that he was not free? It was not just another male replacing him, it was a burgher-citizen of the imperial metropole trouncing the Indio subaltern from the contest for a conjugal partner. It was the freedom of the modern citizen able to alienate/dispose of his/her labor-power in the anarchic market. It was ultimately industrial capitalism blasting the ethnic, geopolitical walls of empire—only to sustain the patriarchal domination of women's bodies.

Leonor Rivera died on 28 August 1893. According to his friend Galicano Apacible, Rizal was shattered, fell into a somnambulistic trance (Rodolfo 1958, 451). While in exile in Dapitan, Rizal met Josephine Bracken (a Eurasian orphan from Hong Kong, Asia's burgeoning commercial center) in February 1895 with whom he fell in love. In March 1895, he wrote his mother to extend hospitality to

Josephine and treat her as a person "whom I hold in great esteem and regard, and whom I should not like to see exposed and abandoned" (Guerrero 1969, 363). This "errant swallow" promised refuge from a hostile world, reviving memories of the relatively free European women whose bodies/minds incited his imagination and fed the subterranean fountainhead of desire. She also functioned as an opportunity to re-affirm his manhood years before the time arrived when he could sacrifice his life to the object of his life's mission: decolonizing and liberating *patria*.

The Shaman's Strip-tease Agency

Accompanying the *estranjera* Bracken, the figure of the vindictive wife (of Uncle Alberto and others) returns to the life of the Dapitan exile in the shape of his research into psychosomatic illness. On 15 November 1895, Rizal wrote the "notes for the study of Philippine medicine" entitled "The Treatment of the Bewitched" (the original title is "La Curacion de los hechizados. Apuntes hechos para el studio de la Medicina Filipina" [Rizal 1999, 138]), ostensibly a scientific account of the etiology of a disease not caused by the usual pathogenic factors.

What is striking is Rizal's description of the female witch, the *manggagaway* (the *mangkukulam*, the male counterpart, seems relatively harmless in casting enchantment), who inflicts a most mysterious, terrible illness, "though fortunately rare." The male mendicant magician is but an "involuntarily malevolent fakir," whereas the female sorcerer bewitches by suggestion. She applies "diabolical arts" the origin of which is really the social milieu, the cultural prejudices, customs and folkways of the time. Rizal diagnoses this type of sorcery as a result of auto-suggestion accompanying delirium, delirium defined by Rizal as "the lack of equilibrium between the perceptions and the conscience, a civil war inside the brain" (1964,180). This delirium is what afflicted Sisa and Juli in one degree or another. This civil war between what Freud would call the reality-principle and the pleasure-principle, between the warring forces of *eros* and *thanatos* in an Oedipalized system, acquires sociohistorical embodiment and performativity in everyday life.

Employing an objectifying stance, Rizal informs us that there are towns in Luzon where all the women enjoy the ascriptive reputation of being a *manggagaway*—a social phenomenon symptomatic of the entire colonial formation and its psychosomatic dynamics. The cure is immanent in its diagnosis. Here is Rizal with the physician's required detachment unable to escape pronouncing judgment on the conduct and reflex behavior of the whole society:

Although some deserve the name for their inexplicable vainglory, for their prattling, for believing that thus they make themselves terrible, nevertheless others are absolutely innocent...A certain air, a behavior somewhat reserved and mysterious, a certain way of looking, infrequent attendance at religious services, and others, are enough to win for an unfortunate woman the reputation of *manggagaway*. She is the she-ass burden of ignorance and popular malevolence, the scapegoat of divine chastisements, the salvation of the perplexed quacks. Mankind also has divine defects among its divine qualities. It likes to explain everything and wash in another's blood its own impurities. The woman *manggagaway* is to the common man and the quack what the resentment of the gods, the demon, the pacts with the devil in the Medieval Age, the plethora of blood, neuroses, and others were to the different ages: She is the diagnosis of inexplicable sufferings (1964, 178).

The witch, more exactly the experience of bewitchment or possession, condenses all the tensions released from the pressures of overlapping conflicts and contradictions of a transitional phase in society, that is, a society undergoing transformative upheavals. Rizal performs the rite of the exorcising, medical shaman. Instead of inveighing and counter-cursing, Rizal's tone is elegiac, oracular, trying to discriminate and at the same time refrain from distinguishing the guilty and the innocent. Nonetheless, as a scientist-physician, he laments the human infirmity of not using reason to analyze and cure the psychic malady. Rizal anticipates

Freud's transvaluation of the soul into the body-phantom registering the impingements of family/society. I submit that this discourse and its context exemplifies a memorable instance of Rizal's historical-materialist sensibility and his ethico-political vocation to bring about a revolution in the national psyche.

Advent of the Babaylan

In the course of his annotating Morga's chronicles, Rizal surely encountered the early missionaries' notes on the *babaylan*. His letter to Blumentritt from Dapitan (dated 20 November 1895) stated that he was "on the way to deciphering the meaning of *babailan*," but nothing more. What I would underscore here is a problematic silence, perhaps a tactical deference on Rizal's part (as ethnologist and physician), not to interpolate in his explanation the case of the *babaylan* or *catalona* stigmatized by the Spanish missionaries into the perverse rubric of the *manggagaway.*

Magic or the instrumentalization of supernatural/psychic power acquires gender differentiation in a colonially stratified milieu. Mostly widows or elderly women, the *babaylan*s were the custodians of folk wisdom in the arts of healing, of divining the future, and the performance of propitiatory rituals. As medical practitioners, astronomers and interpreters of culture, they exercised persuasive control over matters of reproduction and health of the community. They not only presided over the vital rituals of weddings, births, funerals, hunts and war; they also advised the datus and sultans on how to resolve political conflicts and other problems in civic affairs.

With their prestige and their authority over health, fertility and diseases, the *babaylan*s exhibited "the pre-condition to maximize [women's] participation and remain competitive with the men in the other spheres...even to the extent of becoming socially equal, at times, even superior to...the rest of society (Mangahas 1987, 13). Because these religious intermediaries are not organized into sects nor are they in permanent contact with the supernatural realm except during trances or moments of possession, they are more precisely classified as shamanesses (Infante 1975, 194-96).

For the historian Zeus Salazar, the *babaylan* functioned as the third pillar of the economic unit of the *barangay*, the basis for the *bayan* or aggregate of communal settlements. after the *datu, hari* or *lakan* (the political head) and the *panday* (blacksmith). In the process of the military-evangelical conquest of the islands, the *babaylans* were incorporated into church activities as religious women in charge of processions or servants of the convent. Those unable to assimilate, or who resisted the syncreticizing strategy of the church, instigated and supported rebellions such as that led by Sumoroy, by Waray Tupung in Bohol, by the *cofradias* and various messianic organizations including the Katipunan—the formidable example of the revolutionary general Teresa Magbanua easily comes to mind, overshadowing those of Gabriela Silang or Princess Urduja (Salazar 1996). In suppressing such revolts, the Spaniards demonized the *babaylans*, the custodians of the indigenous cultures, reconfiguring them as transgressive witches, *manggagaway*s or *mangkukulam*s (designating men who dare arrogate magical rights or privileges within the animistic frame of tribal beliefs).

It is intriguing to speculate that if Rizal was able to continue his third novel, *Makamisa*, or the narrative entitled "The Ancient Tagalog Nobility," we would probably have for hermeneutic inspection a full-bodied rendering of the *babaylan* in action. Was Teodora Alonso not one avatar of this shadowy nemesis of the patriarchal social contract? Meanwhile, we are left to ponder the vestige of calculating missionary zeal. Behind that prophylactic passage describing the female sorcerer, we witness Sisa and Dona Consolacion distilled in one phenomenal figure—the *babaylan* split into two embodiments. What Rizal enunciates, in general, is a symbolic complex of good and evil coexisting together, what is heretical and impious coalescing in one subject-position. Actually, it is a mirror-image of Rizal as the recalcitrant and transgressive Indio, the unpatriotic expatriate (for the friars) defying the *Comision permanente de censura* by speaking of the true and the real. The witch is Rizal; but the curse is this counter-statement, the doctor's report. Alienated colonial society ascribes the source of its vices, crimes and ignorance to a fraction of the female sex and, in this collective process of purification, acquits male authority of any wrongdoing. Impartiality requires settling accounts with the patriarchs in the church and the bureaucracy (for the European record, see Figes 1970).

Certain sisters of Eve functioned as scapegoat-like Christs, just as the penitent whore Magdalene came about due to "the powerful undertow of misogyny in Christianity, which associates women with the dangers and degradation of the flesh" (Warner 1976, 225; for the communist-oriented views of early Christians regarding women and the family, see Kautsky 1925, 347-354), hence the whore becomes a beloved saint. In Rizal's polyvocal discourse, the realms of the sacred and profane are two halves of the same coin, one an inquiring mirror of the other; hence, the term "divine" operates here as a symptomatic rubric of the religious illusion, the ideological narcotic, that the Enlightenment and the bourgeois revolutions in Europe failed to uproot. It is now Rizal's turn to enlighten his women compatriots, in particular, of the need to liberate themselves from what William Blake called "mind-forged manacles" by their own collective effort and initiative. It is time to re-instate the primacy of personal autonomy and civic solidarity in the arena of everyday life.

The Epistle to the Women of Malolos

Teaching and learning, for Rizal as scholar-researcher in history and ethnology, are indivisibly fused in his role as committed public intellectual (Baron-Fernandez 1980; Ocampo 1998). Study, collective learning, is part of emancipatory praxis that connects human agency and the ecosystem, as Marx implied in his thesis on Feuerbach: "The coincidence of the changing of circumstances and of human activity can be conceived and rationally understood only as revolutionizing practice" (Tucker 1972, 145). His now famous letter to the young women of Malolos, dated Feb. 22, 1889, was elicited by the tireless iconoclastic propagandist-rhetorician, Marcelo H. Del Pilar, while Rizal was preoccupied with annotating Morga's chronicles in the British Museum in London, and also answering the critics of the *Noli* (Ocampo 1988). It was deliberately written in Tagalog at the time when he was also preparing his first article for the reformist journal *La Solidaridad* entitled "Los Agricoltores Filipinos." That intervention may be compared to Karl Marx's two contributions to the *Rheinische Zeitung* on the law against thefts of timber and on the destitution of the Moselle Wine Growers (McLellan 1970, 95-101).

In Rizal's inquiry into the backward conditions of the Filipino farmers, he deplored how the farmer capitalist had to battle not only floods and locusts but also petty tyrannical officials, the constable of the civil guards and the bureaucrats of the court and the provincial government. Already equipped with an astute comprehension of the social relations of production, the political economy of the Spanish colony, Rizal this time focused his critique on the efficacy of the ideological apparatus in sustaining the unrelieved subjugation of the natives, in particular the disciplinary subalternization of women, whom he considered crucial in the formation of children's personality and disposition. In re-visiting Rizal's militant advocacy of a historical-materialist critique of society through his novels and various discourses, contra Constantino (1970) and vulgar Marxists, we can appreciate his singular contribution to humankind's libertarian archive, whatever his other limitations given the circumstances and contingencies of his personal situation and the state of the world in the latter part of the nineteenth century.

The central burden of Rizal's letter is the critique of religion, more exactly, its practice of idolatry and attendant fanaticism which violate "saintliness" defined as obedience to "the dictates of reason." Thus he bewails servitude and "blind submission to any unjust order," since each person can use a god-given reason and will to distinguish the just from the unjust. The role of the dissenting, inquiring conscience becomes crucial for fostering literacy and civic liberty. Positing the radical premise of all humans being born free, with no right to subjugate the will and spirit of another, Rizal urges the use of rational analysis and judgment in all activities—not just in learning Spanish, which for the Malolos women was really a pretext to have access to the mentoring wisdom of Teodoro Sandiko, Rizal's progressive compatriot, whom they wanted as teacher (the petition was eventually granted, but Sandiko was replaced by a person approved by the church).

Rizal's obsession with the need for activating the rational critical faculty is not only a rejection of the stereotypical attributes of modesty, passivity and docility ascribed to women by custom and ecclesiastical authority, but also an attempt to include women as citizens fully qualified to participate in fashioning the "General Will" (in Rousseau's definition) of civil society. While not explicitly mentioning Rousseau, Rizal invokes reason as the primary requisite for self-mastery, for the exercise of moral liberty, which is a precondition for conceptualizing the universal interest of the whole society (Lange 1979; Hendel 1934). Following the Renaissance episteme (in Foucault's construal) of human reason as a reflection of God in the human soul, Rizal is moving to a classic notion of representation being subsumed into an emergent modernist teleology of self-discipline and historical self-consciousness (Foucault 1970). Women need to learn Spanish if only to become doubly visible to the imperial panopticon's surveillance. Rizal adhered to the Socratic maxim, *nosce te ipsum*, as conducing to the true concept of one's self which motivates the dynamic creativity of human intelligence and empowers national progress (1999, 70). Opposing the confinement of women to devalued and debilitating reproductive labor—the expenditure of time and energy in providing nurture and socialization for dependent offspring—Rizal seeks to install women as citizens equal to men in exercising personal autonomy and sympathetic concern for others.

Encountering the School of Life

Rizal's judgment on colonial education in the Philippines is condensed in one sentence in his famous discourse on "the indolence of Filipinos": "The education of the Filipinos from birth until the grave is brutalizing, depressing, and anti-human" (1999, 35). Rizal's studies in Madrid and his friendship with liberal professionals in France, Germany and England no doubt exposed him to both Rousseau's *Social Contract* (1762) and *Emile* (1762). The latter work, *Emile ou de la education*, especially its fifth book, seems to be the source of general romantic ideas (which Rizal absorbed) about childhood and the importance of the constant care of the biological mother—the example of the Spartan mother Rizal cites is used by Rousseau in the first part of the book as a negative example of the perversion of natural feeling (1969, 8). That notion of course dovetailed with the mother-child (Virgin Mary/Jesus) family paradigm in Christian catechism. But in this context, motherhood, for Rizal, was not just a natural attribute but an achieved or acquired social role. Rizal contradicts Rousseau's dualistic belief in associating the female with body/nature/family and the male with mind/citizen/public life. His radical egalitarianism springs from his desire to enroll Filipino women into the ranks of anti-Spanish colonial partisans of the national struggle. Social expectations, not just the family-imposed sexual division of labor, defined the mother as a redemptive teacher.

What is lamentable, for Rizal, is the Filipino woman's failure to be good mothers due to their profligate addiction to gambling, their subservience to the mercenary friars, their zealotry in conforming to reified rituals, and their complacent ignorance: "What sons will she have but acolytes, priest's servants, or cockfighters?" Sisa's gambling husband and her two sons in the convent loom in the background. In suggesting that mothers replace the friars as the fountainhead of moral guidance in the family, Rizal valorizes the agency of mothers as educative/formative forces primarily responsible for shaping the character of their children: "...you are the first to influence the consciousness of man.... Awaken and prepare the will of our children towards all that is honorable, judged by proper standards, to all that is sincere and firm of purpose, clear judgment, clear procedure, honesty in act and deed, love for the fellowman and respect for God" (1984, 327).

Lacking civic organizations outside the family, the mother then becomes the only viable pedagogical alternative to the convent and the church-regulated schools. The native fathers are either conscripted by the government for military service, for unpaid public labor, or occupied in cultivating friar-owned lands. Rizal affirms his faith in the power and good judgment of Filipino women. He believes that Asia is backward because Asian women are ignorant and slavish, whereas in Europe and America "the women are free and well educated and endowed with lucid intellect and a strong will" (128). We know that Rizal admired German women who "are active and somewhat masculine," not afraid of men, "more concerned with the substance than with appearances" (letter to Trinidad Rizal, 11 March 1886; 1993, 223). The figure of Teodora Alonso, the moralizing mother-teacher, is not far behind.

Excursion to Sparta

It is therefore not surprising that Rizal would invoke the civic conscience of Spartan mothers as exemplary. We should first grasp the truth of our situation, he reminds his Malolos audience, perhaps deducing lessons from his own experience: young students lose their reason when they fall in love, and so beware. The passions mislead (to use Spinoza's terms); adequate knowledge of nature is needed to act wisely and responsibly. Moreover, marriage makes shameless cowards of the bravest youth. Rizal then advises women who are married to "aid her husband, inspire him with courage, share his perils, refrain from causing him worry and sweeten his moments of affliction... Open your children's eyes so that they may jealously guard their honor, love their fellowmen and their native land, and do their duty," like the women of Sparta (1984, 330). Rizal extolled Spartan women for giving birth to men who would willingly sacrifice their lives in defense of their homeland.

But Rizal did not mention how that practice was possible because of the rigorous militaristic regimen imposed on the training of Spartan youth, the rigorous routine of the *agelai* or herds (described by Plutarch) in disciplining youth solely for fighting. Ruled by an exclusive ruling caste, Sparta suppressed their serfs (helots) with a permanent military organization (a standing army) and a tribal system of common ownership that prevented the disruptive effects of commodity production, industry and trade using coinage (Thomson 1955, 210-211). The Spartan oligarchy administered the polity's settlement (family estates with serfs) as the prime economic unit based on communal ownership of the soil and local handicrafts. Spartan women were also trained in the *agelai* but "they were free to go about in public; adultery was not punishable or even discreditable; a woman might have several husbands" (Thomson 1968, 190). We are still in a quasi-primitive communal society (somewhat similar to pre-conquest Philippines) where women's work extended beyond the private household. In supervising the production of subsistence and other use-valued goods, women exercised a measure of power and effective rights in the public sphere.

It is clear that Spartan mothers were not the educators Rizal conceived them to be. They did not raise their sons who, at the age of seven, were enrolled in the *agelai* and transferred to the Men's House at nineteen, devoting themselves to military exercises. When married, Spartan men did not live with their wives but visited them clandestinely on occasions; the brides/wives lived with their parents. Women obtained substantial dowries and inherited two-fifths of the land in the absence of their husbands; though excluded from political life, their indispensable position as heiresses and managers of the estates with their ubiquitous helot labor gave them so great an influence that Aristotle spoke of Sparta as a country "ruled by women" (Thomson 1968, 192). Because of the division of labor between the sexes, all adult males served in the standing army while the women administered the family estates. This is what allowed Spartan mothers to sternly judge the performance of their soldier-sons, not their care or nurturance in the private domain of the father-centered home, as Rizal seemed to believe. Education was in the hands of the patriarchal oligarchy of Sparta, not in those of mothers or daughters.

One would expect Rizal to be more knowledgeable or informed, but surely a full substantial description of Spartan society was not his intention. His purpose was to praise Spartan unity—about 9,000 citizens "economically self-sufficient and politically enfranchised" (Anderson 1974, 35)--and their selfless devotion to the defense of their homeland originally conquered from the indigenous Messenians who became state helots. The austere independence of Spartan women thrilled Rizal. In his 1886 letter to his sister Trinidad, Rizal objected to the Filipino women's obsession with clothing and finery attuned to the demands of the marriage market. His instructions at the end reiterate the fundamental virtues of courage, diligence, dignity, and personal autonomy derived from acquiring knowledge ("ignorance is servitude") and the cultivation of intellect, as well as the fulfillment of reciprocal obligations toward others. This repeated exhortation to cooperation and mutual help, a pre-requisite in forging national sentiment (Majul 1961, 73-185), precedes the somewhat peremptory fifth injunction: "If the Filipina will not change her mode of being, let her rear no more children, let her merely give birth to them. She must cease to be the mistress of the home, otherwise she will unconsciously betray husband, child, native land, and all." Beware, parents of Leonor Rivera, Segunda Katigbak, and their sisters—you may be nurturing treacherous wives who pretend to be "mistress of the home" while scheming to deliver husbands, children, homeland, to the enemy. Rizal's parting words seem even more rebarbative: "...may you in the garden of learning gather not bitter but choice fruit, looking well before you eat because on the surface of the globe all is deceit and the enemy sow seeds in your seedling plot."

Experimental Realism

In spite of such shortcomings, the sixth instruction in Rizal's epistle sums up his pedagogical creed: to value intelligence and reason as the enabling principle of equality and solidarity with others. What is reasonable and just is the aim of learning; "to make use of reason in all things" entails the rejection of egotism and the local barbarism of folklore, superstitions, fossilized notions, and anachronistic habits that prevent Filipinos, men and women, from reflecting on their common situation and critically analyzing the impact of movement and change in their collective life. One can detect in Rizal's emphasis on using the "sieve of reason," which is mobilized to grasp "the truth of the situation," an overanxious insistence in developing civic consciousness in women, expressed here as praise for their "power and good judgment," "fortitude of mind and loftiness of purpose," and so on. Here Rizal departs from Rousseau's maxim of differential worth, as well as from the commonsensical, biologistic, liberal notions of the sexes complementing and/or supplementing each other, in treating women as equal to men in being capable of reflective self-development and civic agency in the public sphere. Nonetheless, he subscribes to the French revolution's ideals of equality, liberty and fraternity refracted through the prism of deistic Christianity, "religion within the bounds of practical reason," in Kant's phrase; and of communal honor, Rizal's "self-esteem," in riposte to Fr. Pastell's sardonic attitude (Palma 1949, 235-47)).

Anxious to defend women's honor maligned by the friars and abusive Spanish visitors, Rizal can only retort that Spanish women themselves are not all "cut after the pattern of the Holy Virgin Mary." Since the Malolos women for the most part belonged to the *ilustrado/principalia* class comprised of families with bilateral extensions, Rizal can only abstractly valorize rationality as crystallized in the concrete practice of nurturing children. The household realm is open to affinitive reconstruction. The everyday life becomes a domain of paramount concern. In the process, he appraises women's work in the household as one mediating the relations of the natural and social orders. This domestic work generates what Antonio Gramsci calls "the first elements of an intuition of the world free from all magic and superstition"(1978, 52). Learning, education as the internalized absorption of modalities of empirical investigation and synthetic-analytic reflection, follows Rizal's insight (written from Barcelona circa 1881) that "the knowledge of a thing prepares for its control. Knowledge is power" (1999, 70).

Unlike Sisa, Juli, Salome and women of the peasantry and village artisans, the Malolos assemblage—Rizal surmises—is struggling to overcome the bondage of limited schooling and constricted participation in civic affairs due mainly to the consensual routine of stultifying religious indoctrination. In addition, one has to reckon with paternal surveillance and the long tradition of the *pasyon* and its focus on the mystical transcendence of human suffering. The petition submitted to Gov. Valeriano Weyler to open a night school so that young women might learn Spanish under the progressive mentor Teodoro Sandiko served as the first step in breaking down that bondage of silence and the customary acceptance of women's inferiorization. Their spontaneous agitation may be conceived as their recognition of "necessity" as freedom when they reached out to the propagandists in Madrid and outside their province, a strategic move embodying the radical principle of socializing what was deemed natural and historicizing what was deemed immutable, fated, or predestined. Modernity's historicizing drive has taken over Malolos and the embryonic Filipino diaspora.

Ilustrado Hubris

In the letter, Rizal refined and complicated the analysis of the political economy underlying Filipino women's circumscribed lot to a critique of the church-induced h*abitus* (Bourdieu 1977) of submission and self-abnegation. The reason for this is that in the colonial setup, the ideological propaganda apparatus of the church and its capillary agencies predominated over any liberal reformist tendencies of the arbitrary secular-civilian administration. We can appreciate this better if we keep in mind the ethos of unquestioning obedience and decorum prescribed for women by normative codes and institutional practices distilled, for example, in *Lagda* (1734), a manual of exemplary Christian conduct, and in the widely read text of Father Modesto de Castro, *Urbana at Felisa* (1864), self-described as "an educational moral novel" (Mojares 1983, 82).

The historian Maria Luisa Camagay remarks how the frailocracy abused its authority by sexually exploiting women workers, particularly those applying for the position of *maestra* (teacher) and *matrona* (midwife): "The friar proved to be a bane in the life of Filipino women in the 19th century" (1995, 121). With the employment of more women into the flourishing tobacco factories and in paid domestic services, the power of the frailocracy was gradually demarcated and focused on the women of the *principalia* (e.g. Pia Alba, Maria Clara). It was inflicted on the twenty-one Malolos women, entrepreneurs in farms and urban businesses, who wanted to use part of their free night-hours to develop their intellects and acquire urbane skills.

Rizal was also aware of the enormous weight of Spanish colonial laws—for example, the Spanish Marriage Law of 1870—that subordinated women to the property-owning husband. Applying the doctrine of Roman jurisprudence concerning *patria postestas* with the male *paterfamilias* as absolute ruler, this law together with other Royal Decrees segregated women into *colegios* and *beaterios* that prepared women either for motherhood or the religious life (Feliciano 1996). Rizal's anti-authoritarianism targeted the gendering mechanism of schools, court and bureaucracy, even though by 1781 women were being hired by government-owned tobacco factories, and by 1894 they were being admitted to teaching careers (Camagay 1989, 35). Such recruitment into waged labor in fact simply substituted market compulsion for paternal/church authority. Rizal's praise of prudent resistance to authority, balanced with his stress on "justice [as] the foremost virtue of civilized nations" (in "The Philippines a Century Hence"), distinguishes his implied philosophy of education as part of his agonistic, but also perspectival and thoroughly modern, view of life conveyed to his nephew during his Dapitan exile:

To live is to be among humans and to be among humans is to struggle. But this struggle is not a brutal and material struggle with men alone; it is a struggle with them, with one's self, with their passions and one's own, with errors and preoccupations. It is an eternal struggle with a smile on the lips and tears in the heart. On this battlefield man has no better weapon than his intelligence, no other force but his heart. Sharpen, perfect, polish then your mind and fortify and educate your heart (1993, 375)

Self-discipline as Enlightenment *desideratum* was also what he was trying to articulate in the letter, except that he was more preoccupied with altering the psychophysical disposition of women inured to passivity, obedience and silence, which over-determined the fates of Maria Clara, Juli and Sisa. This accounts for the emphasis on a militarized sense of corporate honor, a warrior ethos distinguished by an ascetic regimen in fulfilling duty and obligations to the community, as if he was trying to convert the feminine *habitus* to a more competitive, adversarial mode (on the ethos of honor, see Ossowska 1970). It seems as though the entrepeneurial Rizal, who engaged in the abaca trade, complained of not earning enough as an eye-doctor, and gambled in the lottery, was more preoccupied with inculcating the aristocratic virtues of the feudal nobility than the bourgeois ethos of regularity, thrift, and profit-motivated cunning. The Spartan model haunts the margins of the epistolary script. He was skipping the stage of hypocritical merchant capitalism (identified with a mercenary priesthood and parasitic native bureaucracy) in favor of a utopian meritocratic arrangement allowing the intelligent an iota of elite privilege while maintaining a semblance of aristocratic decorum.

Although marginal to the plot of the *Noli* (in fact, the whole chapter "Elias and Salome" was excised from the final version), the character Salome displays more affinities with her Malolos sisters, given her relative control over her means of subsistence and her isolation. She is the remaindered kin of the ostracized *babaylan*s. With Elias' decision not to marry her in order to spare her the misery of a wretched family life, she plans to move to the frontier land of Mindoro and join her relatives. Living happily in the wilderness, desiring nothing but health to work and enjoy what is freely offered, not envying the rich girls their wealth, Salome anticipates the nature deity Maria Makiling of Rizal's reconstituted folklore, the p*atria* of the exiled hero.

Salome implores the fugitive Elias to use her dwelling: "It will make you remember me...When my thoughts go back to these shores, the memory of you and that of my home will present themselves together. Sleep here where I have slept and dreamed...it would be as if I myself were living with you, as if I were at your side" (*Noli* 216-17). The narrative conjures their consensual togetherness, their carnal liaisons, their mutual belonging, in fantasy or compensatory wish-fulfillment that is invariably women's mode of transcending quotidian misfortunes. What imbues space with charismatic import and historic significance is women's work, affection, care; hence Rizal's extreme anguish that mothers perform their nurturing, child-rearing task well in fashioning autonomous citizens. Natural law takes precedence over positive man-made laws.

Envisioning the Totality

On December 31, 1891, shortly after completing the *Fili,* Rizal wrote to Blumentritt that the reformist *La Solidaridad* is no longer his chosen battlefield. With the sharpening crisis of the Spanish empire, the arena had shifted to the Philippines (Zaide 1984, 213). His family had suffered an irreversible catastrophe when they were evicted by the Dominican friars from the Calamba hacienda the year before and his relatives persecuted. His sojourn in Hong Kong marked his definitive turn to an insurrectionary, separatist solution for the colony.

His two epistolary political testaments dated 20 June 1892, and his founding of the *Liga Filipina* on his arrival in Manila in June-July 1892, herald the beginning of Sisa's and Juli's "vengeance," a recovery of the primal outrage. Melancholia's shroud may have fallen on Rizal in Dapitan, but underneath it all the victims of colonial tyranny are gathering for a coven/covenant to exorcise the demonic plague. Rizal's own view of the synoptic, ruminatory years of his Dapitan exile may be discerned in the "structure of feeling" (Williams 1977) behind his statement to Fr. Pablo Pastells: "I am at present at the enactment of my own work and taking part in it" (1930-38, 63). The present fuses the past and future in one intuitive act of Rizal's sensibility, his personal judgment of the totality of his experience universalized by sharing its moral import with others capable of empathy, reciprocity, or vicarious identification with neighbors and fellow protagonists. Modernity, characterized by the hegemony of capitalist norms, revisits like a vampire the archaic layers of the communal past since it cannot answer objectively the inescapable ethico-political and essentially moral questions of what is true justice, virtue, and the good life from a global/cosmopolitan perspective (Gramsci 1985).

A more historicized appraisal of Rizal in this age of terrorism would thus move the center of inquiry to the Dapitan years following the Hong Kong interlude, the contacts with the plebeian/proletarian strata interested in the *Liga*, and the *Liga*'s resonance (Olsen 2007). It is the moment of timely reckoning. By exposing the limits of Simon's anarcho-utopian idealism and Padre Florentino's eschatological wish-fulfillment, Rizal moved to engage in its existential ramifications the Sisa-Salome nexus embedded in the carnivalesque world of colonial Philippines deprived of any *nomos* or transcendental authority. Rizal anticipates the postmodern predicament of the dissolution of a meaningful world in vacuous finance-capitalism.

Women's vengeance against patriarchal nihilism lies submerged in Rizal's communicative gesture to the Malolos contingent, potential cadres or partisans of the nascent Katipunan-led revolution. This outreach mobilizes emergent and residual historical forces in a dialectical trajectory of canceling the negative (mystifying ideologies and practices) and salvaging the mother's body/place as the site of the subject's reconstitution. This itinerary of changes in his thinking provides a seismographic organon for comprehending Rizal's radical critique, his theory of transforming *patria* and the regenerative delirium of its victims into a counterhegemonic historic bloc (Quibuyen 1999), the matrix of all subversive insurgencies. This will permanently nullify the common prejudice that Rizal should be dismissed as an American-installed icon and replaced by the action-driven Bonifacio, thereby unwittingly admitting pragmatic expediency and a cultic voluntarist spontaneism as the criteria of populist hero-worship.

We can sidetrack Simon's conspiracy in the *Fili* and focus instead on a utopian moment in Rizal's narrative. By this I do not mean the utopian-socialist trend of Saint Simoun, Fourier and Owen criticized by Engels (1978) in *Socialism: Utopian and Scientific* (published in French 1880, with English translation in 1892). While Rizal may have absorbed ideas surrounding the debates around both Engel's polemic and the earlier 1848 *Communist Manifesto*, his general philosophical outlook owes its bearings more to the classical Greek and Roman tradition inflected by Cicero, Duns Scotus, and Thomas Aquinas, then subsequently re-oriented by the secularizing Renaissance and by the Enlightenment (Voltaire, Diderot, Rousseau); and radicalized later by such mavericks as the Marquis de Condorcet, the theoreticians of the Paris Commune of 1871, William Godwin, and Mary Wollstonecraft—see, in particular, her *A Vindication of the Rights of Woman* issued in 1792 (Mitchell 1984 68-72; Beauvoir 1952, 136-37).

In his commentary on Morga's *Sucesos*, Rizal's vindication of Filipino women's honor (reiterated in the Malolos epistle) finds eloquent testimony. It is a return to the past before mother-right was completely annulled, when the self-sustaining security of the *gens* (clan) had not completely yielded to the vulnerable, isolated nuclear family dominated by the property-owning male. Women still participated in socially necessary labor (Sisa's horticultural knowledge is a survival) in the domestication of crops and household management, before the complete dehumanization of mother-oriented communal ties in the subjugated colony. Because Filipina women are not a burden to the husband, Rizal argues, she does not carry a dowry: "the husband does not take a heavy burden or the matrimonial yoke, but a companion to help him and to introduce thrift in the irregular life of a bachelor" (1999, 26). Even though the native woman before the Spanish conquest "represents a value for whose loss the possessor [parents] must be compensated, she was never a burden on her parents or husband; European families, however, seem to be in a hurry to get rid of their marriageable daughters, with mothers frequently playing a ridiculous role in the sale of her daughter." The sale and purchase of Filipino women is not a custom in the past, according to Rizal's ethnological research (but there are widespread exceptions, as documented by Teresita Infante [1975]):

The Tagalog wife is free and respected, she manages and contracts, almost always with the husband's approval, who consults her about all his acts. She is the keeper of the money, she educates the children, half of whom belongs to her. She is not a Chinese woman or a Muslim slave who is bought sometimes from the parents, sometimes at the bazaar, in order to lock her up for the pleasure of the husband or master. She is not the European woman who marries, purchases the husband's liberty, initiative, her true dominion being limited to reign over the salon, to entertain guests, and to sit at the right of her husband (1999, 26).

Allowing for a certain overstatement in the position of women in pre-colonial times, it is accurate to state that in the communal stage of the *barangay*, the division of socially necessary labor and with it, the specification of gender roles, had not yet been affected by commodity production and the circulation of exchange values. To the degree that women participate integrally in productive work, as well as with the reproductive labor of the household, they enjoy a measure of equality with men. As soon as private property (land, labor, commodities) becomes the dominant logic of the social order, male supremacy and monogamy prevail, supplemented by adultery and prostitution (Leacock 1972). When women were excluded from productive work and confined to kitchen and boudoir, their participation in political and public affairs also ended. With the male partner absent or emasculated, Sisa and Salome enjoyed a latitude of activity, a degree of autonomy, not shared by Maria Clara, Paulita Gomez, or Leonor Rivera.

We may hypothesize that this is one of the reasons why Rizal found Josephine Bracken, whom he celebrated in his "ultimo adios" as "dulce extranjera," a breath of fresh air. It was a temporary respite from the surveillance of the solicitous mother and his female siblings. Even though she was obedient, meek, and did not answer back when Rizal lectured, she belonged to the European/Western "race" and was not averse to engaging in manual labor in Dapitan. Clearly, Rizal was not threatened by her, as he was by Nelly Boustead, Gertrude Beckett or the business-minded Viennese temptress; she was an orphan, with "nobody else in the world but me [Rizal]" (1993, 417). Despite appearances, she harbored an excess beyond his control. In the hours before his death, Rizal wrote his family, asking forgiveness and requesting them to "Have pity on poor Josephine" (1993, 439). After her marriage to Rizal and his execution, Bracken actively participated in the revolutionary war led by General Emilio Aguinaldo (Ofilada 2003), perhaps realizing a fragment of Rizal's image of those formidable Spartan mothers he invoked as guides to the promised land.

Intervention from the Mountain: A Millenarian Project?

Whatever impasse of contradictions undermined his life, Rizal never gave up *amor patria*, the "most heroic and most sublime human sentiment," He celebrated this obsessive nostalgia for the homeland in his first propagandist contribution to *Diariong Tagalog* (20 August 1982) when he landed in Barcelona on his first sojourn in Europe. Rizal is rhapsodic in proclaiming his adoration for the Motherland which inheres in every human: "She has been the universal cry of peace, of love, and of glory, because she is in the hearts and minds of all men, and like the light enclosed in limpid crystal, she goes forth in the form of the most intense splendor" (1962, 15). She is incarnate in fantasy, in the mythical figures associated with the natural surroundings, with the soil and rivers of the native land: "And how strange! The poorer and more wretched she is, the more one is willing to suffer for her, the more she is adored, the more one finds pleasure in bearing up with her" (1962, 16).

Geographical space, the occupied territory, becomes a concrete, lived place; it mutates into a libidinally charged locus of pleasure and self-sacrifice. When the motherland is in danger, the more intense the desire to come to her aid; the motherland symbolizes all those kin you have lost, the fountainhead of dreams, but also where "true Christianity" abides. Rizal finally identifies what he would later address, in his farewell poem, "mi Patria idolatrada, dolor de mis dolores/Querida Filipinas," with Christ "on the night of his sorrow." Our sacrifices will revive the dying, suffering homeland (in the martyr's allegorical rendering), now taking the persona of Josephine Bracken--"mi amiga, mi alegria"--now that of Maria Makiling and her eternally recurrent metamorphosis. This is the antithesis to the imperial masculinist high-bourgeois nationalism of the oppressor metropoles so lustily condemned by arrogant pundits and academic stars of the global North, self-aggrandizing sophists so proud of their erudition and their always infallible opinions on what's wrong with the world.

It is instructive that Rizal, instead of dwelling on the didactic fable of Malakas and Maganda (coopted by the hired publicists of the Marcos dictatorship 1972-1986) born together as a sign of gender parity, calls our attention to the legend of Maria Makiling. She concentrates in her figure the diverse manifestations of the nature-fertility goddess throughout the archipelago. While inhabiting the borderline between nature and civilization, she remained a virgin, "simple and mysterious like the spirit of the mountain." Initially, she favored humans with her grace and bountiful beauty; but when she was deceived by her earthly lover, she took revenge. Rizal suggests that perhaps she was infuriated by the attempt of the Dominican friars "to strip her of her domains, appropriating half of the mountain" (1962, 107).

The goddess rebuked her human lover when he took another bride: "inasmuch as you had not courage either to face a hard lot to defend your liberty and make yourself independent in the bosom of these mountains; inasmuch as you have no confidence in me, I who would have protected you and your parents, go; I deliver you to your fate." Since then, the goddess never again showed herself to humans, no matter how hard they searched for her "along the famous ascent that the friars called *filibustera*," according to Rizal. The original harmony of humans and the ecosystem is sundered by predatory acquisitiveness, by the exploitation of nature to yield subsistence, so "neither the enchanted palace nor the humble hut of Mariang Makiling could be glimpsed" again (1962, 110).

And so did Salome abandon her home in the forest, so did Sisa and Juli depart from the fallen world of Padre Camorra, Padre Damaso and Padre Salvi, of Dona Consolacion, the alferez and *guardia civiles*—the outposts of the crumbling Spanish empire. In the 1892 Hong Kong letter, he declared: "I desire, furthermore, to let those who deny our patriotism see that we know how to die for our duty and for our convictions. What matters death if one dies for what is loved, for the country, and for the beings that are adored?" (Palma 1949, 351).

Rizal is sacrificing himself on the temple steps, a programmatic gesture inaugurated in the *Noli*'s preface. Sisa's vengeance arrives here with the martyr's apostrophe to the Motherland to pray for "our unhappy mothers who in bitter sorrow cried," rendering judgment on those condemned to languish in a world where slaves bow before the oppressor, where faith kills. At the end of his 1884 eulogy to the painters Juan Luna and Felix Resurrecion Hidalgo, Rizal offered a paean to Filipino parents after delivering a challenge to their children: "The furrow is ready and the ground is not sterile!" (quoted in Zaide and Zaide 1984, 74).

What Is To Be Done?

It was in the same year, 1884, when Rizal became involved in the university student insurrection in Madrid, that Engel's epoch-making book, *The Origin of the Family, Private Property and the State,* was published. In mapping the evolution of the family, Engels noted that Spartan women occupied a much more honored position and exercised greater sexual freedom than anywhere else in antiquity during that period. This was because pairing marriage, not monogamy, was still practised in Sparta; private property of land and household goods was unknown. Like Rizal, however, Marx and Engels to a lesser degree were still deeply "imbued with the rationalist tradtion of Plato and More to allow free play to all psychosexual desires as authentic needs" in the way Charles Fourier (or the Marquis de Sade) did in his utopia of amorous "passionate refinement" (Manuel and Manuel 1979, 710). Before and during his first sojourn in Spain in 1882-85, Rizal had already digested Rousseau, Voltaire, Schiller and Victor Hugo. but not Fourier. To be sure, he knew the Russian Nihilist movement and probably Proudhon and Bakunin, and indirectly Marx and Engels, given the contentious ambience of anarchists, syndicalists, and utopian socialists saturating Paris, London, Brussels. Berlin, Vienna, and other cities he visited from 1886 to 1887, and later from 1888 to 1892. In this context, Rizal might plausibly be called the first Filipino high modernist during the twilight of the Spanish empire.

Four years before his death, Rizal responded to his Jesuit "inquisitor" Fr. Pastells: "My sole wish is to do what is possible, what is in my hands, the most necessary. I have glimpsed a little light and I believe that it is my duty to teach it to my countrymen" (1999, 93). In being fully comprehended and assayed, the realm of necessity, of fate, becomes the terrain of freedom; thus, as he earlier observed in "The Philippines a Century Hence," "every country meets the fate that she deserves." Whether we deserve Rizal and the ideals he fought for, is a question whose answer may already be immanent in the ongoing struggles in the open green fields around us. Uncannily serendipitous, inhabiting the borderland between patriarchy and matrilineality, the surname "Rizal" is not found in the clan genealogy. The patronymic "Rizal" was given by an unnamed provincial governor to distinguish the dangerous Mercados of Calamba, a gratuitous addition that fulfilled in the ripeness of time its prophetic signification in designating "a field where wheat, cut while still green, sprouts again" (Guerrero 1969, 19).

REFERENCES

Aguilar, Delia. 1988. *The Feminist Challenge: Initial Working Principles towards Reconceptualizing the Feminist Movement in the Philippines.* Manila: Asian Social Institute.
----. 1999. *Toward a Nationalist Feminism.* Quezon City: Giraffe.
Anderson, Benedict. 2005. *Under Three Flags.* New York and London: Verso.
Anderson, Perry. 1974. *Passages from Antiquity to Feudalism.* New York: Verso.
Arcilla, Jose. 1991. *Rizal and the Emergence of the Filipino Nation.* Quezon City: Ateneo de Manila University
Baron-Fernandez, Jose. 1980. *Jose Rizal: Filipino Doctor and Patriot.* Quezon City: Manuel Morato.
Beauvoir, Simone de. 1952. *The Second Sex.* New York: Vintage Books.
Benjamin, Walter. 1977. "Conversations with Brecht." *Aesthetics and Politics.* London: New Left Books.
Bernad, Fr. Miguel. 1998. "The Trial of Rizal." *Philippine Studies* 46 (First Quarter): 46-72.
Bigelow, Herbert S. 1899. "Jose Rizal, Filipino Patriot." *The Public* I (March 18). In Jim Zwick, ed., *Anti-Imperialism in the United States, 1898-1935.*
Bonoan, Raul J. 1996. "Jose Rizal, Liberator of the Philippines." *America* (December).
Buck-Morrs, Susan. 2003. *Thinking Past Terror.* London and New York: Verso.
Bourdieu, Pierre. 1977. *Outline of a Theory of Practice.* London: Cambridge University Press.
Camagay, Ma. Luisa. 1989. "Women Through Philippine History." In The Filipino Woman in Focus, ed. Amaryllis Torres. Bangkok, Thailand: UNESCO, reprinted in 1995 by the UP Office of Research Coordination.
----. 1995. *Working Women of Manila in the 19th Century.* Quezon City: University of the Philippines Press.
Caudwell, Christopher. 1971. *Studies and Further Studies in a Dying Culture.* New York: Monthly Review Press.
Chant, Sylvia and Cathy McvIlwaine. 1995. *Women of a Lesser Cost: Female Labour, Foreign Exchange and Philippine Development.* Quezon City: Ateneo University Press.
Constantino, Renato. 1970. *Dissent and Counter-Consciousness.* Quezon City: Malaya Books, Inc.
Craig, Austin. 1913. *Lineage, Life and Labors of Jose Rizal.* Manila: Philippine Education Co.
Dizon, Alma Jill. 1998. "Felipinas Caliban: Colonialism as Marriage of Spaniard and Filipina." *Philippine Studies* 46 (First Quarter): 24.45.

Ebert, Teresa. 1996. *Ludic Feminism and After*. Ann Arbor, MI: The University of Michigan Press.
Eliade, Mircea. 1958. *Patterns in Comparative Religion*. New York: Meridian Books.
Eviota, Elizabeth Uy. 1992. *The Political Economy of Gender*. London: Zed Books.
Feliciano, Myrna. 1996. "The Filipina: A Historical Legal Perspective." In *Women's Role in Philippine History: Selected Essays*. Quezon City: University Center for Women's Studies.
Feria, Dolores. 1968. "The Insurrecta and the Colegiala." In *Rizal: Contrary Essays*, ed. Petronilo Daroy and Dolores Feria. Quezon City: Guro Books.
Fernandez, Jose Baron. 1980. *Jose Rizal: Filipino Doctor and Patriot*. Manila:
Manuel L. Morato, publisher.
Figes, Eva. 1970. *Patriarchal Attitudes*. New York: Fawcett World Library.
Foucault, Michel. 1970. *The Order of Things*. London: Tavistock Publications.
Goody, Jack. 1998. *Food and Love*. London and New York: Verso.
Gramsci, Antonio. 1978. "From 'In Search of the Educational Principle." In *Studies in Socialist Pedagogy*. Ed. Theodor Mills Norton and Bertell Ollman. New York: Monthly Review Press.
-----. 1985. *Antonio Gramsci: Selections from Cultural Writings*, ed. David Forgacs and Geoffrey Nowell-Smith and translated by William Boelhower. Cambridge, MA: Harvard University Press.
Guerin, Daniel. 1970. *Anarchism*. Introduction by Noam Chomsky. New York: Monthly Review Press.
Guerrero, Leon Maria. 1969. *The First Filipino: A Biography of Jose Rizal*. Manila: Vertex Press Inc.
Gurvitch, Georges. 1971. *The Social Frameworks of Knowledge*. New York: Harper Torchbooks.
Haug, Frigga. 1999. "On the Necessity of Conceiving the Utopian in a Feminist Fashion." In *Necessary and Unnecessary Utopias*, ed. Leo Panitch and Colin Leys. *Socialist Register 2000*. Suffolk, UK: Merlin Press.
Hays, H.R. 11958. *From Ape to Angel*. New York: Capricorn Books.
Heller, Agnes. 1999. *A Theory of Modernity*. New York: Blackwell.
Hendel, Charles W. 1934. *Jean-Jacques Rousseau: Moralist*. New York: The Bobbs-Merrill Co.
Hogan, Patrick Colm. 2000. *Philosophical Approaches to the Study of Literature*. Gainesville, Florida: University Press of Florida.
Howard, Dick. 1977. *The Marxian Legacy*. New York: Urizen Books.
Howells, William Dean. 1901. "The Editor's Easy Chair." *Harper's Monthly Magazine* CII (April): 802-806.
Ileto, Reynaldo. 1998. *Filipinos and Their Revolution*. Quezon City: Ateneo de Manila University Press.

Infante, Teresita R. 1975. *The Woman in Early Philippines and Among the Cultural Minorities*. Manila: Unitas Publications.
Jameson, Fredric. 1988. "Metacommentary." In *The Ideologies of Theory*, Vol. 1. Minneapolis, MN: University of Minnesota Press.
Joaquin, Nick. 1977. *A Question of Heroes*. Makati: Ayala Museum.
----. 1988. "Small Beer: Love Scene." *Philippine Daily Inquirer* (Feb. 13): 11.
Kautsky, Karl. 1925. *Foundations of Christianity*. New York: International Publishers.
Kramer, Paul. 2006. The Blood of Government. Chapel Hill, NC: University of North Carolina Press.
Kristeva, Julia. 1986. *The Kristeva Reader*. New York: Columbia University Press.
Lahiri, Smita. 1999. "Writer, Hero, Myth and Spirit: The Changing Image of Jose Rizal." Available at: <http://www.einaudi.cornell.edu/SoutheastAsia/outreach/SEA Pbulletin /bulletin_fa99/lahiri_fa99.html>
Laqueur, Walter, ed. 1978. *The Terrorism Reader*. New York: New American Library.
Lange, Lynda. 1979. "Rousseau: Women and the General Will." In *The Sexism of Social And Political Theory*, ed. Lorenne Clark and Lynda Lange. Toronto: University of Toronto Press.
Leacock, Eleanor B. 1972. "Introduction." Frederick Engel, *The Origin of the Family, Private Property and the State*. New York: International Publishers.
Lopez, Salvador P. 1968. "Maria Clara—Paragon or Caricature?" In *Rizal: Contrary Essays*, ed. P. Daroy and D. Feria. Quezon City: Guro Books.
Macey, David. 2000. *The Penguin Dictionary of Critical Theory*. New York: Penguin Books.
McLellan, David. 1970. *Marx Before Marxism*. New York: Harper and Row.
Mangahas, Fe. 1987. "From Babaylan to Suffragettes: The Status of Filipino Women from Pre-Colonial Times to the Early American Period." In *Kamalayan: Feminist Writings in the Philippines*, ed. Pennie Azarcon. Quezon City: Pilipina.
Manuel, Frank and Fritzie Manuel. 1979. *Utopian Thought in the Western World*. Cambridge, MA: Harvard University Press.
Majul, Cesar A. 1961. "On the Concept of National Community." In *International Congress on Rizal*. Manila: Jose Rizal National Centennial Commission.
----. 1974. "Three thinkers: how they moved men and events." *Archipelago* I, 11 (November): 8-13.
Martinez-Ramirez, Miguel A. 1961. "El Dr. Jose Rizal Glorificado en Cuba." In *Rizal*. Manila: Jose Rizal National Centennial Commission.

Marx, Karl. 1956. *Selected Writings in Sociology and Philosophy.* Ed. Tom Bottomore. New York: McGraw-Hill Book Company.
----. 1970. *Critique of Hegel's 'Philosophy of Right.'* New York: Cambridge University Press.
----. 1975. *Early Writings.* New York: Vintage Books.
Marx, Karl and Fredrick Engels. 1973. *Marx and Engels on Literature and Art*, ed. Lee Baxandall and Stefan Morawski. Milwaukee & St. Louis: Telos Press.
----. (1844) 1975. *The Holy Family.* Moscow: Progress Publishers.
----. 1978. *The Marx-Engels Reader*, ed. Robert Tucker. New York: W.W. Norton.
Matibag, Eugenio. 1995. " 'El Verbo del Filibusterismo': Narrative Ruses in the Novels of Jose Rizal," *Revista Hispanica Moderna* (December): 250-64.
Mies, Maria. 1986. *Patriarchy and Accumulation on a World Scale: Women in the Internationa Division of Labor.* London: Zed Books.
Miller, Stuart Creighton. 1982. *Benevolent Assimilation: The American Conquest of the Philippines, 1899-1903.* New Haven: Yale University Press.
Mitchell, Juliet. 1984. *Women: The Lost Revolution.* New York: Pantheon Books.
Mojares, Resil. 1983. *Origins and Rise of the Filipino Novel.* Quezon City: University of the Philippines Press.
Nakpil, Carmen Guerrero. 1980. "The Filipino Woman." *Asian and Pacific Quarterly* XII, 2 (Summer): 10-18. First printed in the *Philippines Quarterly*, 1952, and reprinted in Carmen Guerrero Nakpil, *Woman Enough and Other Essays* (Quezon City, 1973).
Ocampo, Ambeth. 1990. *Rizal Without the Overcoat.* Manila: Anvil Publishing. Available at
----. 1998a. *The Centennial Countdown.* Manila: Anvil Publishing.
----. 1998b. "Rizal's Morga and Views of Philippine History." *Philippine Studies*, 46.2 (1998): 184-214.
Ofilada, Macario. 2003. *Errante Golondrina.* Quezon City: New Day Publishers.
Oizerman, T. I. 1981. *The Making of the Marxist Philosophy. Moscow*: Progress Publishers.
Olsen, Rosalinda N. 2007. "Rizal and the Myth of the Golden Pancake." *Bulatlat* vii. 5 (March 4-10).
Ossowska, Maria. 1970. *Social Determinants of Moral Ideas.* Philadelphia: The University of Pennsylvania Press.
Palma, Rafael. 1949. *The Pride of the Malay Race.* New York: Prentice Hall.
Peirce, Charles Sanders. 1998. *The Essential Peirce.* Bloomington and Indianapolis: Indiana University Press.
Pinoy Abrod. 2004. "Panalo sa Pag-iingles sa London." Vol. 1, No. 2: 5.
Quibuyen, Floro. 1999. *A Nation Aborted.* Quezon City: Ateneo University Press.

Radaic, Ante. 1999. *Jose Rizal Romantiko Realista.* Tr. Trinidad O. Regala. Quezon City: University of the Philippines Press.

Rafael, Vicente. 2003. "Foreignnesss and Vengeance: On Rizal's *El filibusterismo.*" In *Southeast Asia Over Three Generations,"* ed. James Siegel and Audrey Kahin. Ithaca: Southeast Asia Program, Cornell University.

Ranciere, Jacques. 2004. *The Politics of Aesthetics.* New York: Continuum.

Retana, Wenceslao. 1979. "Rizal—An Appraisal." In Rizal. Manila: National Historical Institute. Prologue to "El Filibusterismo," Terera Edicion, Madrid, Imprenta de Heinrich y Cia, 1908.

Richardson, Jim. 2006. "Academic Anarchy." *Journal of Contemporary Asia* : 532-44.

Rizal, Jose. 1930-1936. *Epistolario Rizalino*, ed. Teodoro Kalaw. Volumes 1-5. Manla: Bureau of Printing.

----. 1930-38. "Rizal to Blumentritt, London, Nov. 8, 1888." In *Epistolario Rizalino.* Vol V, Part 1. Ed. Teodoro M. Kalaw. Manila: Bureau of Printing.

----. 1950. *The Young Rizal.* Translated by Leon Ma. Guerrero. Manila: Bardavon Book Co.

----. 1961. *The Rizal-Blumentritt Correspondence.* Manila: Jose Rizal National Centennial Commission.

----. 1962. "Mariang Makiling." In *Rizal's Prose.* Volume 3, Book Two. Manila: Jose Rizal National Centennial Commission.

----. 1962. "Mi Retiro," in *Rizal's Poems.* Tr. Encarnacion Alzona. Centennial Edition. Manila: Jose Riaal Centennial Commission, 1962.

----. 1964. Miscellaneous Writings of Dr. Jose Rizal. Vol. VIII. Manila: National Heroes Commission.

----. 1974. "Reflections of a Filipino." In Filipino Nationalism 1872-1970, ed. Teodoro Agoncillo. Manila: R.P. Garcia Publishing Co.

----. 1984a. "To The Young Women of Malolos." In Gregorio Zaide and Sonia Zaide,, *Jose Rizal.* Manila: National Bookstore. The original Tagalog text is available at: <http://joserizal.info/Writings/Other/Malolos-tagalog.htm>

-----. 1984b. "Si Barrantes at ang Dulaang Tagalog." In *Ang Ating Panitikan,* ed. Isagani Cruz and Soledad Reyes. Manila: Goodwill Trading Co. Originally published in 1889.

----. 1993. *Letters Between Rizal and Family Members 1876-1896.* Manila: National Historical Institute.

----. 1999. *Quotations from Rizal's Writings.* Translated by Encarnacion Alzona. Manila: National Historical Institute.

----. 2004. *Noli Me Tangere.* Translated by Soledad Lacson-Locsin. Manila,Philippines: Bookmark.

-----. 2004. *El Filibusterismo.* Translated by Soledad Lacson-Locsin. Manila, Philippines: Bookmark.

Rodolfo, Agustin. 1958. "Rizal as a Propagandist." *The Diliman Review* (April-December): 416-57.
Rousseau, Jean-Jacques. 1969. *Emile*. Tr. B. Foxley. New York and London: Macmillan.
Salazar, Zeus. 1996. "Ang Babaylan sa Kasaysayan ng Pilipinas." In *Women's Role in Philippine History: Selected Essays*. Quezon City: University Center for Women's Studies.
Schumacher, John. 1978. "Rizal the Revolutionary and the Ateneo." Manila Review 17 (December): 65-73.
San Juan, E. 1999. *Filipina Insurgency*. Quezon City: Giraffe.
----. 2011. *Rizal In Our Time*. Revised ed. Manila: Anvil Publishing.
Thomson, George. 1955. *The First Philosophers*. London: Lawrence and Wishart.
----. 1968. *Aeschylus and Athens*. New York: Universal Library.
Tucker, Robert C. 1972. *The Marx-Engels Reader*. New York: W.W. Norton.
Unamuno, Miguel de. 1961. "Rizal." In *Rizal*. Manila: Comision Nacional del Centenario de Jose Rizal.
Warner, Marina. 1976. *Alone of All Her Sex: The Myth and Cult of the Virgin Mary*. New York: Vintage Books.
Williams, Raymond. 1977. *Marxism and Literature*. New York: Oxford University Press.
Zaide, Gregorio and Sonia Zaide. 1984. *Jose Rizal: Life, Works and Writings of a Genius, Writer, Scientist and National Hero*. Manila: National Bookstore.
Zizek, Slavoj. 2008. *Violence*. New York: Picador.
Zwick, Jim, ed. 1992. Mark Twain's Weapons of Satire. Syracuse, NY: Syracuse University Press.

RIZAL THE FEMINIST

A Book Review of *Sisa's Vengeance*

by Francis C. Macansantos

E. San Juan, Jr. was one illustrious young poet of the sixties, showing mastery of the medium in both Filipino and English. He has since reinvented himself as scholar of literature and culture, in America where he is based. With a Ph.D. from Harvard and professorships *emeritus* from several universities in the U.S., he is deemed an intellect of the first rank in literary and philosophical circles abroad. But just like Rizal, our first intellectual, San Juan is an exile, opting though to return to his country in the form of the books and articles he has written elsewhere, scholarly vessels that contain riches of insight on his motherland's history, culture, and politics. Some who admire his poetry would prefer verse, but from his published offerings it seems as though he has hung up his lyre.

In prose, however, the rapport he has kept up with his motherland has been fervidly dynamic. Her freedom from post-colonial chains is the constant poem in this scholar's heart. He reminds us of that other illustrious *viajero,* the controversial novelist, Dr. Jose Rizal.

And it is obvious that like most Filipino intellectuals, San Juan can never drop the subject of Rizal or his continuing relevance to the idea of liberation. What he does reject is the notion that we need to choose between Bonifacio and Rizal, one against and excluding the other. Indeed, he even sets aside discussion (postponed for another book, perhaps?) on Rizal's refusal to join the revolution, preferring instead to emphasize the hero's achievement in conceptualizing an authentic ideological guide to freedom.

In *Sisa's Vengeance*, San Juan takes up and evaluates the views of practically all the major Rizal biographers and commentators, pointing out their shortcomings. He takes special exception to *Under Three Flags* by Benedict Anderson, whose assessment of Rizal lowers his stature as political thinker to that of a "mere moralist and novelist." On good authority (of Jim Richardson who exposes Anderson's numerous errors) he attacks Anderson's "ignorance" and lack of conceptual rigor.

But it is only towards the later chapters of *Sisa's Vengeance* that San Juan fully discloses his main theme (and to most of his macho countrymen a startling one): that the proof of his authenticity as revolutionary is his principled belief in and his fervent advocacy of women's rights.

It comes to light in the book's latter chapters that for San Juan, the cause of women's liberation is the *sine qua non* to any authentic movement for human liberation. An authentic vision of social change requires a profound understanding and staunch espousal of the cause for women's rights.

Media has tended to present Rizal as a fickle playboy with a girl in every port. Such popular representations flatter the self-image of Filipino machos. But San Juan's sensitively scrupulous view yields to us a more respectful, even at times diffident man in love—often a victim of heartbreak, all despite Maximo Viola's account of Rizal's presumed encounter with a Viennese woman of the streets.(Rizal, in fact, was actively involved in the rehabilitation of sex workers.)

Rizal idolized his mother who was an exceptionally gifted and cultured person, and he was made aware by his studies in London of Morga's *Sucesos*, of the high social status of women of the Philippine islands before the Spanish conquest. It was in London in the midst of his research on Morga that he wrote—upon the request of M.H. del Pilar—his rightly famous letter (written in Tagalog) to the women of Malolos proclaiming their right to education and their duty transmit their learning to their children.

Apart from these women, his mother, and those whom he was linked with amorously, Rizal had other—albeit imaginary—women: Maria Clara, Sisa, Juli, Doña Consolacion, Salome, and others—the women of his novels. Sisa, especially, is central to San Juan's meditation on Rizal's character, as it is she who embodies the victimization of women and of the motherland. After establishing the necessary link between the patriarchal system and all oppressive (because profit-oriented) systems, San Juan adroitly transforms Rizal's arguably feminist position into a fulcrum to elevate and authenticate his revolutionary status.

Indeed, San Juan's readings of Rizal's literary works recommend themselves directly to students and scholars of literature. *Sisa's Vengeance* provides a plethora of insights into Rizalian texts that are a fitting reward for any reader who has plowed through the rather difficult--often specialized—prose. Such oases, or epiphanies (pun intended) are surely traces of a poetic sensibility.

[*Francis C. Macansantos is a Baguio-based writer,who writes poetry, essays and fiction in English and Chabacano, his native language. He is a Palanca award winner and an NCCA Writers Prize awardee. His latest book, Balsa: Poemas Chabacano, was recently launched at Ateneo de Zamboanga, where he received the Most Outstanding Alumnus of the Year award in December 2011.]*

ABOUT THE AUTHOR

E. SAN JUAN, Jr. is emeritus professor of English, Comparative Literature, and Ethnic Studies from several U.S. universities. He received his A.B. from the University of the Philippines and his A.M. and Ph.D. from Harvard University. He has taught at the University of California; Brooklyn College of CUNY; University of Connecticut; Trento University, Italy, Tamkang University, Taiwan; and Washington State University. He was recently a fellow of the W.E.B. Du Bois Institute, Harvard University; Fulbright professor of American Studies at Leuven University, Belgium; and fellow of the Rockefeller Study Center at Bellagio, Italy. Among his recent books are: *Racism and Cultural Studies* (Duke UP), *Working Through the Contradictions* (Bucknell UP); *US Imperialism and Revolution in the Philippines* (Palgrave); *In the Wake of Terror* (Lexington); *Balikbayang Sinta: An E. San Juan Reader* (Ateneo U Press); *From Globalization to National Liberation* (University of the Philippines Press); *Critique and Social Transformation* (Edwin Mellen Press); *Critical Interventions* (Lambert Academic Publishing, Saarbrucken, Germany); and *Rizal In Our Time* (revised edition, Anvil Publishing).

Printed in Great Britain
by Amazon